A Future that's Bigger than the Past

A Future that's Bigger than the Past

Catalysing Kingdom Communities

The Chalmers Lectures, 2019

Samuel Wells

CANTERBURY
PRESS
Norwich

© Samuel Wells 2019

First published in 2019 by the Canterbury Press Norwich
Editorial office
3rd Floor, Invicta House
108–114 Golden Lane
London EC1Y 0TG, UK
www.canterburypress.co.uk

Canterbury Press is an imprint of Hymns Ancient & Modern Ltd
(a registered charity)

Hymns Ancient & Modern® is a registered trademark of
Hymns Ancient & Modern Ltd
13A Hellesdon Park Road, Norwich
Norfolk NR6 5DR, UK

Scripture quotations are from the New Revised Standard Version of
the Bible, Anglicized Edition, copyright © 1989, 1995 by the Division
of Christian Education of the National Council of the Churches of
Christ in the USA. Used by permission. All rights reserved.

Where indicated, scriptures are quoted from the Good News Translation
published by The Bible Societies/HarperCollins Publishers Ltd UK
© American Bible Society, 1966, 1971, 1976, 1992.

British Library Cataloguing in Publication data

A catalogue record for this book is available
from the British Library

978 1 78622 177 3

Typeset by Manila Typesetting Company

For Geoffrey Brown

'Those who believe in me will do what I do –
yes, they will do even greater things.'
John 14.12, Good News Translation

Contents

Preface

A book like this shouldn't really have a single author, and so the business of these introductory remarks is to highlight those without whom there would have been no St Martin-in-the-Fields, no HeartEdge movement, no imagination of a future that's bigger than the past.

I am grateful to the Most Revd Derek Browning, Moderator of the General Assembly of the Church of Scotland 2017–18, and the Revd Dr George Whyte, Principal Clerk, and their committee for the invitation to give the Chalmers Lectures at Greyfriars Kirk, Edinburgh, in September and October 2019, and for their explicit request that the lectures should concern the theology and methods of HeartEdge, and the confidence in the movement that this request shows. I am indebted also to Richard Frazer and his team at Greyfriars for their warm welcome.

I want to give credit to Jonathan Evens and Andy Turner, who established HeartEdge, and to Neville Black and Martin Sergeant, who in different ways played crucial roles in envisioning and resourcing the idea. I am grateful for early adopters, too many to name, but including Richard Frazer, Lucy Winkett, Mike Branscombe, Giles Goddard, Christopher Woods, Andy Goodliff, David Mayne, Erica Wooff, Dan Tyndall, Hilary Oakley, Ruth Gouldbourne, Simon Woodman, Jo Loveridge, Jonathan Sedgwick, Bob Lawrie, Mark Kinder, Tim Vreugdenhil and James Hughesden, and for the steering group, which has included several of the early adopters but also Duncan McCall, Andrew Caspari, Ali Lyon and Peter Keegan.

Special thanks go to Katy Shaw and her team in generating resources and developing strategy, to Andrew Earis, Richard Carter, Allyson Hargreaves and Tim Bissett, whose work has pioneered much of the energy behind HeartEdge, and to the wider team at St Martin-in-the-Fields, including Pam Orchard, Katherine Hedderly, Chris Franklin, Chris Braganza, Catherine Jackson, Chris Burford, Cathy Reid Jones, the PCC and the company board, and all who, as lay volunteers, staff and clergy, have made St Martin's a place where beautiful things happen every day.

The work of St Martin's today stands on the shoulders of countless committed, talented and faithful people over many decades, back to 1914 and beyond. We may say with the letter to the Hebrews, 'All of these died in faith without having received the promises, but from a distance they saw and greeted them' (11.13). If two names were to be singled out as representatives of them all, they might be Geoffrey Brown, whose courage and enterprise, together with that of those who worked alongside him, saved St Martin's from a financial precipice in the late 1980s, and for whom the St Martin's of today is perhaps the best memorial; and Nicholas Holtam, under whose leadership the whole site was completely renovated and upgraded, and whose team's work set the stage for the next chapter in this remarkable story.

I want to mention those not already named who have guided, inspired, refined, enriched or contributed to parts of the book or argument, including Ched Myers, Greg Jones, Jonathan Kearney, Giles Goddard, Peterson Feital, Walter Brueggemann, Maureen Knudsen Langdoc, Kelly Johnson and Russell Rook. Particular thanks to Rebekah Eklund for detailed comments on the manuscript and to Georgie Illingworth who, as well as assisting Jonathan and Andy, was a great help with the appendix and with turning the written word into audio-visual lectures.

I first used the phrase 'a future that's bigger than the past' in 1994 in Wallsend, North Tyneside, when presiding at a service of prayer and dedication after a civil marriage. It struck me that for this particular couple to enter marriage again, having vividly seen its more challenging dimensions, was the triumph of hope over experience in a rather inspiring way, and promised a future unclouded by the storms previously known. It occurred to me at the time that the phrase alluded to the way, for Christians, what God has in store is always more than we have already known.

But when it came to establishing an ecumenical movement for church renewal in this generation, the phrase struck me again, because the one thing I felt the need to set aside was a widespread, almost universal, lament that the church had lost its hold on the imagination of the public at large, and that something vital, irreplaceable and glorious had been irretrievably lost, such that what lay ahead was its inevitable demise. To me this assumed an unjustifiably rose-tinted view of the living-memory past and an unnecessary yet self-fulfilling perspective on the foreseeable future. The word 'bigger' may be clumsy, but it's designed to be provocative. It's the phrase I most associate with the distinctive quality of St Martin-in-the-Fields – an institution, fundamentally a church, which, unusually in our time, truly believes that in Christ the future is always bigger than the past. Long may it be so.

Introduction:

A Vision for Church Renewal

The church is getting smaller; and the church is becoming narrower. Those who regularly attend worship are fewer; and the church's reputation and energy are becoming associated with initiatives that are introverted and often lack the full breadth of the gospel. The two questions this situation evokes are, 'How do you feel about this?' and 'What are you doing about it?' This book is written to address this situation and answer those questions. It does so by placing the situation in a larger social and economic context and by offering a carefully thought-through and assiduously tested answer to the questions. This introduction offers a beginning to addressing the situation and to answering the questions.

What this book is about

Reforming church

The ideas that permeate this book emerged in reflecting on the five-hundredth anniversary of the Protestant Reformation. 'Reformation' refers to the process by which (1) a new idea (2) takes revolutionary hold on the imagination of a generation, resulting (3) in a transformation in political, social or religious institutions. The key to the sixteenth-century Reformation was the uncovering of a new and exhilarating understanding of salvation, namely justification by grace through faith. Martin Luther believed this doctrine had always been there, being embedded in Ephesians 2, and maintained that it had been obscured by the church, which, through its accretions over the centuries, had more or less replaced it with a notion of salvation through works – of which the sale of indulgences was but the most egregious symptom. For Luther, the doctrinal changes were primary, whereas for the Reformed theologians John Calvin and Huldrych Zwingli, and even more so for the Radical Reformers, institutional realignment was essential; thus under their authority the threefold order of bishops, priests and deacons was swept away. But for all Protestants, the key social development was the putting of the Bible in the vernacular in the hands of ordinary lay Christians for devotional and ethical use, and no longer keeping it solely in Latin and restricting it to the liturgical use of the clergy.

If we are to mean anything in our generation by invoking the term 'reformation', I think it makes sense to do so if we follow that threefold pattern, beginning with (1) the new idea, perceiving how it (2) changes assumptions, attitudes and actions, and then anticipating and outlining (3) the new institutional forms it assumes and requires. So these opening remarks take that threefold shape.

The new idea

'I came that they may have life, and have it abundantly' (John 10.10). Christians don't have to look far for a mission statement for the church. Living abundant life: that's what the Father intends, the Son embodies, the Spirit facilitates. Christians are called to live in such a way that gratefully *receives* the abundance God is giving them, *evidences* the transformation from scarcity to abundance to which God is calling them, *dwells* with God in that abundant life, and *shares* that abundance far and wide. Jesus is our model of abundant life; his life, death and resurrection chart the transformation from the scarcity of sin and death to the abundance of healing and resurrection; he longs to bring all humankind into reconciled and flourishing relationship with God, one another, themselves and all creation. Discipleship describes inhabiting that abundant life.

Ministry involves building up the church to embody that abundant life. Mission names the ways that abundant life is practised, shared and discovered in the world at large.

So far so good: nothing not to like. So, as doctors say, what seems to be the problem? Well, around 1860 something important began to change. People started to stop believing in hell. It was on both philosophical and moral grounds. They 'did the maths' and worked out that while 10 million years of roasting in hell seemed in order for the most unspeakable sinners, 10 million is less than a drop in the ocean compared to eternity. Meanwhile, the agonies and horrors of hell seem hard to reconcile with the grace and mercy of God. Once one realizes eternity is infinitely longer than 50 billion years, there is simply no imaginable sin or even evil that merits eternal punishment. And a God who doesn't grasp that seems a very different sort of God from the God revealed in Jesus Christ.

So that's the new idea.[1] Salvation is not fundamentally to be conceived as enabling people to escape from the labours of life and the horrors of hell to the halcyon joys of heaven. Jesus did not fundamentally come to redirect us from judgement and oblivion to safety and sublime bliss. Instead, God always purposed to be in relationship with us and foster our relationship with one another and creation. Jesus came to embody that purpose, to encounter and challenge all that inhibits it, to withstand and demonstrate the overcoming of those obstructions, and to restore that purpose in perpetual promise.

How does this idea change our theological and social imagination?

When you're pondering salvation, there are three questions to ask. What is the problematic nature of our human condition? In what jeopardy does that condition place us? And, what solution is God offering us? (You could say there's a fourth question, namely, how does Jesus bring that solution about? – but I'm not going to concern myself with that question here.)

Using these questions, let's look at what I suggest are three broad ways of conceiving of salvation. According to the first version of salvation,

- the human problem is death;
- the jeopardy we're placed in by death is that we each stand on the brink of being permanently deprived of our identity, existence, relationships, experiences and joys; and
- the solution God offers us in Jesus is the gift of eternal life.

According to the second version,

- the human problem is sin and evil;
- the jeopardy we're placed in by sin and evil is that at the moment of our death we face the prospect of God's judgement and the possibility of short-term, long-term or permanent punishment; and
- the solution God offers us in Jesus is the forgiveness of sins.

According to the third version,

- the human problem is isolation;
- the jeopardy we're placed in by isolation is that we fail to come anywhere near realizing our own potential or enjoying the gift of one another; and
- the solution God offers us in Jesus is to show us the heart of God and the paradigm of abundant life.

I'm suggesting that the church's vocation lies in putting much greater emphasis on this third conception, of receiving, evidencing, dwelling in and sharing abundant life.

I'm not saying that sin and death have ceased to be damaging and fearful aspects of the human predicament. I'm saying that rather than being regarded as accumulating a catalogue of transgression, sin is better understood as impeding abundant life; and meanwhile that the goal of discipleship is to develop a relationship with God so profound that it transcends suffering and can't be terminated even by death. So by saying it's time we recognized we've stopped believing in eternal hell, I'm arguing that Christianity is fundamentally about cultivating the assets of grace and joy and only secondarily about eradicating the deficits of sin and death.

One prayer that's written deep in my heart is this: 'God of time and eternity, if I love thee for hope of heaven, then deny me heaven; if I love thee for fear of hell, then give me hell; but if I love thee for thyself alone, then give me thyself alone.'[2] This prayer discloses four problems with the evading-hell model of church. This model

- *diminishes God* by seeing the Trinity not as an end to be glorified in itself but largely as a means to rescue us from torment or oblivion.
- *impoverishes the world* by seeing it as a prison to be escaped rather than a theatre, playground and garden to be enjoyed.
- *misrepresents the church* by understating the church's shortcomings while overstating the deficiencies of the world.
- *depletes the church* by depriving it of and blinding it to the abundant gifts God has to give it through the world.

It takes a while to comprehend just how much of a revolution in the Christian theological imagination arises when we quietly let go of the evading-hell model of church. There are two closely related dimensions.

- First, the central purpose of church needs a rethink. Church can no longer be principally a mechanism for delivering people from the perils of damnation to the joys of the Elysian Fields. God is no longer principally an instrument for conveying us upstairs rather than downstairs. God is not fundamentally a means to the end of securing our eternal survival and bliss. God isn't, in fact, a means to any end. God is, instead, an end: as the prayer puts it, 'If I love thee for thyself alone, then give me thyself alone.' The central purpose of the church is no longer to reconcile people to God so their eternal

5

salvation will cease to be in jeopardy; it is to invite people to enjoy God just as God enjoys them. God embraces them for their own sake, not for some ulterior purpose: evangelism means inviting people to embrace God likewise.

- Second, the attitude of church to world needs to change. From the evading-hell perspective, the world is characterized by the flesh and pervaded by the devil, so worldly existence is largely to be spent escaping the earthly realities around us and encouraging others to do so. The church offers sanctuary, heavenly medicine, protection and training for avoiding earthly snares and temptations. But a different view of God leads to an alternative understanding of the world. No longer is life about dodging the flesh of this world in order to merit the spirit of the next. Now the world has a validity of its own. All has not been lost in the Fall. The Holy Spirit is doing surprising, exuberant and plentiful things in the world. The church is called not simply to guide people's escape from the world, but to celebrate creation, enjoy culture and share in flourishing life. The evading-hell approach tends to concentrate on how to convey to the maximum number of people the specific benefits secured by Christ's passion, so as to ensure those people seek those benefits and are accordingly delivered unto heaven. By contrast the abundant-life approach seeks to shape communities whose habits and practices anticipate and portray the life of God's kingdom.

What new institutional forms does this assume and require?

I'm suggesting that our doctrine has, whisper it quietly, changed – or, as Roman Catholics would say, developed. The trouble is that *the structures of our churches have lagged behind*. For the most part our churches are still set up to achieve the evading-hell goal. They still take people out of the world for an intense hour or two a week to be transported to heaven and thus to be restored or fuelled or inspired to face the challenges of their lives. They tend to define spirituality in tension with, and superior opposition to, materiality. They regard true devotion as being taken away from the world or resting in silent seclusion from the world. They have a banking model of mission that assumes we need to stock up on scriptural and theological knowledge and then in mission communicate as much of that knowledge as we can to unwary people who, by definition as part of the world, are characterized only by their lack of such knowledge and the godliness that we take to come with it.

I want to outline briefly three ways in which I believe the institutional character of the church might be reformed in order more fully to reflect and advance this notion of salvation as abundant life. For simplicity, I'm going to call them ABC.

'A' stands for assets. Seventy years ago in this country the government became the church. In establishing the welfare state, it took over all the practical things in education, health and welfare that the church used to do. The church said hallelujah. But it didn't realize it had started to build in its own obsolescence. It created a dualistic dichotomy by which the state looked after the body and the church looked after the soul. Now the state is deciding it doesn't want to be the church any more – it's too expensive, because demographic changes mean the number of people paying taxes is no longer much higher than the number receiving benefits, and the system only works in times of prosperity when, ironically, it's least needed. In the last 20 years, the churches have increasingly reinserted themselves in social welfare; but without a clear theological rationale.

I suggest that the role of government is to address deficits – historically the five evils William Beveridge identified in his famous 1942 report – Ignorance, Squalor, Want, Disease and Idleness. But government is useless at cultivating assets. It's the role of civil society in general and the church in particular to cultivate assets of relationship, creativity, partnership, compassion and joy.[3] For too long the churches have been seen lingering on the edge of the public square, offering little in the way of practical help but with a perpetual tendency to judge, criticize and condemn. At worst the church has lapsed from advocacy for the disadvantaged into lobbying like any other interest group for its own advantage.

The church's role in mission should be the same as it is in discipleship and ministry: to cultivate assets and thereby foster and advance abundant life. It makes no sense for the church to become institutionally involved in areas that require specialist expertise or demand economies of scale and rigorous even-handed distribution, like benefit payments. But it makes every sense for the church to witness to its faith in an incarnate Lord who cares for the material reality of people's lives by building community capacity and enhancing training, education, personal development and creative expression so as to enable individuals and neighbourhoods to flourish. Social engagement isn't an add-on to the core business of worship; it's a form of worship, because in the kingdom disciples are humbled, moved and transformed as they stumble into the surprising places and come face to face with the disarming people in whom the Holy Spirit makes Christ known.

The churches have on the whole done a fair job of social service and social advocacy. But the next dimension, of social entrepreneurship, has been neglected. Social service *providers* like Mother Teresa make the world 'more equal, safer, healthier and . . . better'. They take direct action; but they 'leave the existing system in place while seeking to reduce its negative effects'. Social *advocates* like Martin Luther King work indirectly, 'advocating for legislative changes that can transform the environment in question'. Social *entrepreneurs* 'both take direct action and seek to transform the existing system. They seek to go beyond better, to bring about a transformed, stable new system that is fundamentally different' from what preceded it.[4]

The church should be about modelling and making possible forms of social relationship not found elsewhere. It should not be about keeping teenagers occupied and entertained until eventually and inevitably they lose interest; it should be about capturing their imagination with a form of social practice so authentic and so inspiring that instead of being embarrassed that their church is so off the pace they are attracted by a community whose form of relating is striding boldly ahead of their culture rather than dragging grudgingly behind it. Christianity caught on in the second and third centuries because it created institutions that gave people possibilities and opportunities the rest of the world had yet to imagine. That's what Christianity was originally: a revolutionary idea that took institutional form. That's what it needs to become again. Here's a question: when did secular business schools start studying and teaching social entrepreneurship? The answer is, about the time the church stopped studying and practising and being the best example of it.[5]

'B' is for blessing. Churches in this country were in most cases built with the benefaction of the local squire to address the spiritual aspect of an established community. In practice, in addition to their many aesthetic and liturgical qualities, they operated to a significant degree as an assertion of existing hierarchies and an imposition of social control. Today they are in danger because the noblesse are not so obliged when it comes to replacing the roof every second generation and providing a third son of the household to be the vicar, and the community of disciples is not sufficiently extensive or wealthy or generous as to step in. But these church buildings should never have come to be seen simply as set-apart places of retreat to facilitate the once-weekly elevation of the souls of the few to the throne of heaven. They must be regarded as places of encounter for the whole neighbourhood, with a mission to be a blessing to anyone and everyone who resides or spends time there. The architecture may be glorious, and there's no reason why the external appearances need to change significantly, but the priority internally should be as a place that advances abundant life locally, within which liturgical worship should take an honoured but not unduly privileged place. If a local church finds itself in decline, but has lost its vocation to be a blessing to every member of its community, it has only itself to blame.

Finally, 'C' is for community. For many churches, C has only meant communion – in the narrow sense of a formal liturgical act of worship that embodies and expresses the faith and convictions of disciples. But community means more than that. In the historical context I've described, churches could largely rely on there being such a thing as a local community, and the church could capitalize on its rhythm and stability by inviting it to share in the round of Christmas, Mothering Sunday, Easter, Rogation, the parish fête and Harvest. But today such community is much harder to come by, and the church needs to step in with a holistic practice of its own. That means, as I have said, assuming its congregational life will be augmented by a charitable arm, whether entirely voluntary or a mixture of salaried and voluntary, which in most cases will be concerned primarily with cultivating the community's assets. It means, as I have described, making its building available and encouraging its use for cultural and artistic events that foster creativity, expression and beauty, thus portraying flourishing life. And it means in many cases developing sources of income based on the site that offer employment and generate profit and make the organization sustainable.

What I'm describing is transforming church buildings – underused, seen as moribund, and a drain on resources (in other words a metaphor for the whole church) – into dynamic centres of abundant life, receiving, evidencing, dwelling in and sharing forms of social flourishing and being a blessing to their neighbourhood.

I'm not talking about a revolution, but I suspect I am talking about a reformation. And at root I'm describing what happens when we cease to use God as a device for acquiring the ultimate goods we can't secure for ourselves, and start to adore and imitate the God who in Jesus models, offers and advances abundant life, now and for evermore. That's what this book is about.

What inspired this book

In March 2006, I heard a lecture by Ched Myers on the parable of the shrewd manager in Luke 16.1–9. That lecture struck me deeply, and two months later I preached a sermon inspired by it, called 'It's the Economy, Stupid'.[6] Six years later when I came to be vicar of St Martin-in-the-Fields and, for the first time in my life, found myself in a leadership role in relation, among other things, to a significant business venture, I reflected on the questions raised in that sermon. What I offer here is an adapted and extended commentary on the passage that explains the philosophy I brought into my role in relation to that business and why I quickly came to believe that the business should be seen not simply as instrumental to the work of St Martin's but integral to it. It's hard to describe the impetus for establishing a national movement, part of which is intended to foster the closer connection between commerce and congregational life, without setting forth the ideas articulated below, beginning with the parable itself.

Jesus said to the disciples, 'There was a rich man who had a manager, and charges were brought to him that this man was squandering his property. So he summoned him and said to him, "What is this that I hear about you? Give me an account of your management, because you cannot be my manager any longer." Then the manager said to himself, "What will I do, now that my master is taking the position away from me? I am not strong enough to dig, and I am ashamed to beg. I have decided what to do so that, when I am dismissed as manager, people may welcome me into their homes." So, summoning his master's debtors one by one, he asked the first, "How much do you owe my master?" He answered, "A hundred jugs of olive oil." He said to him, "Take your bill, sit down quickly, and make it fifty." Then he asked another, "And how much do you owe?" He replied, "A hundred containers of wheat." He said to him, "Take your bill and make it eighty." And his master commended the dishonest manager because he had acted shrewdly; for the children of this age are more shrewd in dealing with their own generation than are the children of light. And I tell you, make friends for yourselves by means of dishonest wealth so that when it is gone, they may welcome you into the eternal homes.' (Luke 16.1–9)

The story of the manager comes in four scenes. In scene one, a very wealthy man employs a manager. The manager has the use of everything the rich man has. In scene two, the rich man hears that the manager is squandering the property. Straight away the rich man fires the manager: this is a cut-throat world. But there's a moment of grace: before he clears out his office, gets a sympathetic pat on the back from his staff and lifts from his desk the family photos, the manager has the opportunity to visit all the rich man's clients to settle up their accounts. In scene three, the manager has a bright idea. He knows he's too lazy to be working class and too proud to be underclass. He starts writing off the debts of the rich man's major creditors. It's too late to make money, but it's not too late to build social capital. He starts making friends – people who will be pleased to see him after he loses his job, as he surely will. In scene four, the rich man comes face to face with the manager; and the rich man says, 'Good for you, you were in a mighty big hole and you got out of it simply by being generous. You realized that generosity is the best investment. You're better at this than I am.' The story contains an electric shock at the end. What might it mean to hear a rich man say, 'I can see you've discovered the secret of real wealth – generosity.' It's some challenge, to register that generosity is the best investment.

Ched Myers reads the story as a lesson in economics. For him, in scene one, we have a stark picture of economic realities. One man has a huge amount of money. But scene two tells us that this economy is dominated by sudden mood changes, by gossip and anxiety. Everyone is just a puppet on the rich man's string. In scene three, the manager says to himself, 'I wonder whether this is the only kind of economy going. I wonder whether in this desperate moment it might be time to try a novel approach.'

Myers looks at the Greek root of the word 'economics' – *oikonomia* – household management. Economics means putting your house in order. But what if you've lost your home, lost your job, lost your shirt in a cut-throat economy? The manager says to himself, 'I have decided what to do so that, when I am dismissed as manager, people may welcome me into their homes.' The same phrase is repeated at the end of the story. Welcome me into their homes. In other words, when my economics is up the creek, it may be time to invest in somebody else's. When my household is bankrupt, it may be time to think about other people's households. It's time to change economies.

Drawing on Wendell Berry's essay 'Two Economies', Myers points out that the scriptures have words to name the two economies portrayed in this story.[7] The economy of the rich man is called mammon. It's fine as far as it goes, but the problem is it doesn't go very far. It only includes certain people, only buys certain things, only lasts a limited length of time. Mammon is fundamentally the economy of scarcity. It is the world in which there is not enough to go round. Mammon means I must use all my energy making sure that of the limited amount of cake, at least I get enough on my plate. There's also a name for the other economy, the economy of the manager after he's been fired. The biblical word for that economy is manna. Manna is the food God gave to the Hebrews in the wilderness: always more than they needed. It only dried up when they tried to take two days' supply at once. Manna is for everybody, gives what money can't buy, and never expires. Manna is the economy of abundance. It is the currency of the kingdom of God. The secret of happiness is learning to love the things God gives us in plenty. The name for those things is manna.

What happens in scene three of this story is that the manager gives up trying to squeeze people for a living and starts making friends instead. He realizes the friends are more important than the money – or even the job. He moves from mammon to manna, from an economy of scarcity and perpetual anxiety to an economy of abundance and limitless grace. In scene four, the rich man realizes that the manager's economy is bigger than his. The rich man can spot a winning formula. He doesn't say, patronizingly, 'You're a lousy manager but at heart you're a decent guy.' He does say, 'I can see my economy is smaller than yours. You're the one who's living in the great economy. I need to learn from you.' The manager's economy of friendship is just plain bigger than the rich man's economy of debt. The manager has left the rich man's economy, and the investments he's made have made him rich in a way the rich man can only begin to imagine.

But there's also a Christological dimension that emerges if we examine the structure of the story. It's a story about a governor who is about to make his servant pay the price for all the shortcomings of his estate. But he holds off for a bit to see if that servant can transform the estate to become more nearly as the governor would wish it. And because of the servant the governor sees an estate and an economy he'd never seen before. Put another way, the story is about a God who was set to punish his servant for the sins of the world. But he held off a while and the servant used the time before the end of the world to show what grace could do. And God said, 'This economy' (the economy of the servant of God, or we might say the Son of God) 'is really my economy, the economy I shall adopt.' Fundamentally, the manager is Jesus. The economy of relationship described in the parable is the kingdom of God made possible by Jesus' intercession at the right hand of the Father. Jesus literally is the abundance of God, the one who uses the time offered by God's patience in delaying the world's end to transform scarcity into abundance and inaugurate the economy of grace. We're not the manager in the parable. We're the people who were once debtors. Jesus is the manager who has marked down our debt. Jesus is the one who's turned us from resentful and entitled antagonists and nervous and anxious sinners into joyful and thankful friends. And we live in the joy of God's abundance by welcoming Jesus into our homes, knowing that he will welcome us eternally into his.

So far from being a warning against church involvement with business, this parable encourages disciples to think of business as at least an analogy, and quite possibly a fine example of how they are to choose which economy they are going to live in. Will they live in the small economy, the economy that is fine as far as it goes, but turns out not to go very far – the economy that only includes certain people, only buys certain things, only lasts a limited length of time – the economy of anxiety and scarcity? Or will they live in the great economy, the economy where the only use of wealth is to make friends and set people free, the economy in which you are never homeless and you cannot be destitute because you have spent your time and money making friends who will always welcome you into their homes – the economy of abundance, where generosity is the best investment? The parable suggests if they live in the small economy they will spend their life fearing for their job, their livelihood, their reputation, their health, their family, their life itself. If they live in the great economy they won't fear anything. They'll have the things that money can't buy and they'll know the things that hardship and even death can't take away from them. They'll have learned to love the things God gives in plenty. They'll be living truly abundant life.

The final lesson of the story for our lives and our pockets is that there's no such thing as giving or buying or hoarding or saving: there's only investment. And generosity is the best investment.

At the heart. On the edge.

Since the 1980s, in the West, social progress has lagged behind economic progress. Living standards have improved but solidarity and empowerment have been neglected. Economists who have assumed growth was everything missed the fact that care, belonging, trust, identity and agency have been diminishing. The result is an increasing sense of powerlessness and isolation.

The social role of the church lies precisely in these areas so badly neglected by economic policies for the last 40 years. A gospel that advocates a personal faith, assures a welcome in a heaven to come and emphasizes individual discipleship colludes with a socio-economic dismantling of community and belonging. A gospel that longs for heaven to come to earth, that is built on mutual solidarity, that discovers gifts in the stranger, and seeks to be a blessing to a whole society, is offering the world what it most desperately needs.

Once, churches were among many associations that advanced mutual self-help and promoted social good. The church was tempted to retreat and create a special, 'spiritual', realm that was its own preserve. Now almost all such associations – uniformed organizations, Rotary clubs, unions – are in retreat. Meanwhile, social bonds are in a process of huge cultural change. This is a wonderful opportunity for the holistic, body-and-soul vision of the church to be renewed and embodied. There is a unique opportunity for such a national movement of renewal in church and society.

One of the themes of this book is how church renewal isn't simply about the church addressing its shortcomings and flourishing in the ways of God's kingdom. It's also about the church recognizing its role in civil society against the backdrop of significant global challenges, notably questions of human flourishing, particularly artificial intelligence and the future of work, and social cohesion, especially the prevalence of social media and the rise of populist reaction to globalization. A healthy response to such issues is primarily dependent on the suitability and adaptability of institutions within civil society – institutions small enough to retain a personal touch, but large enough for their example to come to wider attention and attract imitation. Rather than teaching the rest of society how to live, or monitoring social norms to ensure they conform to gospel standards, as perhaps some in the church have hitherto understood their role, this is about offering a dynamic example and provoking imitation.

I have come to regard St Martin-in-the-Fields, a church on Trafalgar Square in central London, as one such institution with the character and dynamism to exhibit what qualities agents in the civil economy require, and what goods such institutions generate. In the thirteenth century, St Martin's was a small church in the fields between the city of Westminster to the west and south and the city of London to the east. It became the royal parish church when the king feared the encroachments of plague-ridden worshippers near the Palace of Westminster, and a new church was built in the sixteenth century, in which George Herbert worshipped in the seventeenth century. In 1726, looking for a way to legitimize the union of Hanover and Britain in 1714, George I built the third St Martin's, whose blend of architectural styles also affirmed the union of Scotland and England in 1707. In the nineteenth century, Trafalgar Square was created and the National Gallery and Nelson's Column erected, and St Martin's attained an even greater prominence as the oldest building, now located on the corner of the square.

In 1914 Dick Sheppard became vicar. His ministry to soldiers heading towards Charing Cross station and the trenches began the church's association with homeless people. He made the first religious broadcast in 1924; close ties with the BBC made St Martin's famous nationally and (through the World Service) internationally. The creation of the Academy at St Martin in the Fields in 1958 made St Martin's as famous for its music as for its social outreach, and the inception of a commercial enterprise in 1987 enabled financial sustainability. A huge makeover, completed in 2008, transformed and upgraded the site. The institution continues to grow in profile and operations. It describes itself as 'a community of hope, reimagining church and society through compassion, commerce, culture and congregational life' (the 4Cs).

The vision of the community is 'At the Heart. On the Edge.' St Martin's is at the heart of London and at the heart of the Establishment. Theologically, St Martin's exists to celebrate, enjoy and embody God being with us – the heart of it all. This is not a narcissistic notion that we are the heart, but a conviction that God is the heart and we want to be with God. Meanwhile, the word 'heart' refers to feeling, humanity, passion, emotion. It means the arts, the creativity and joy that move us beyond ourselves to a plane of hope, longing and glory. It means companionship, from a meal shared in the cafe or a gift for a friend perhaps bought in the shop. At the heart means not standing on the sidelines, telling the government what to do, but getting into the action, where honest mistakes are made but genuine good comes about, where new partners are found and social ideas take shape.

The *edge* refers to the edge of Trafalgar Square, looking over its splendour and commotion, pageant and protest. But theologically the word 'edge' speaks of the conviction that God's heart is on the edge of human society, with those who have been excluded or rejected or ignored. St Martin's isn't about bringing those on the imagined 'edge' into the exalted 'middle'; it's about saying we want to be where God is, and God's on the edge, so we want to be there too. Being on the edge does mean facing the cost of being, at times, on the edge of the church. Some of the issues we care deeply about are not areas of consensus in the church. We aim to practise what we believe is a true gospel, where we receive all the gifts God is giving us, especially the ones that the church has for so long despised or patronized. But the 'edge' also means a leading edge, perhaps a cutting edge with an outstanding music programme, a green footprint and an eye for issues around disability. In particular, it means a commercial enterprise that's integrated into the life of the church community and, rather than simply being a source of funds, is at the forefront of the congregation's interface with London's civil economy.

It's not that unusual for a church to run a business, although most outsource the operations to an external provider. It's not at all unusual for a church to run a significant arts programme, although not on the scale of 170 ticketed and 230 free concerts a year, with major art commissions and exhibitions. It's not unusual for a church to be so closely associated with a homeless centre or in some other way to engage seriously with a pressing social issue through voluntary and professional action. What makes St Martin's unique is that it does all three of these things all the time, while still maintaining a flourishing congregation and a wider public ministry, including large-scale memorial and other poignant worship services, a lively lecture programme and frequent BBC broadcasts. The whole project involves around 200 members of staff and at least 300 volunteers. Perhaps a million people come on to the site each year, of whom around 600,000 eat in the cafe and 100,000 attend a concert. The ministry and building upkeep are funded by the commercial surplus, congregational giving, small change from visitors and benefaction from major donors; the social outreach is made possible by grants, local authority contributions, private donations, and proceeds from the annual BBC Radio 4 Christmas Appeal with St Martin-in-the-Fields, which has been running for over 90 years. There are two national networks, one of institutions seeking to dialogue with, and in some respects replicate, the St Martin's model, and another of homeless support workers seeking to share best practice and experience.

The uniqueness of St Martin's lies not so much in its geographical location, royal connections and broadcasting profile, nor in the extent and breadth of its operations, but in the way its activities and commitments catalyse and enhance each other. The following dimensions illustrate this central insight.

1 The congregation is committed to an unapologetic, practical, aspirational and inclusive form of Christianity. In a plural world, few in the public square are prepared to articulate a true telos or vision for the ultimate purpose of the world and human life within it. Meanwhile, those who do, often have a narrow perspective that foments hostility or fosters resentment. For St Martin's, Christianity means generosity, gratitude and humility; goodness, beauty and truth; all issuing from the love of God in Christ. There are few things the world needs more than the articulation of a telos that makes room for all and approaches the stranger with expectation and gentleness.

Because congregational life at St Martin's has for a hundred years been associated with engagement with the poorest in society, it has avoided the three main perceptions that have led people to become distant from institutional

Christianity: a sense that it was too heavenly minded to be any earthly use, a view that it was judgemental and only concerned with its own righteousness, and an observation that it was hypocritical and failed to practise what it preached. The practical commitment of St Martin's is widely known and earns it an enviable reputation among those who would seldom consider attending a worship service.

Being aspirational and inclusive is a rare combination, because diversity is widely thought to be a concession that inevitably entails a lowering of aesthetic and/or social standards. But St Martin's champions diversity not out of pity or even justice but from a recognition that, to be the best it can be, it needs the involvement of every strand of society. There is no 'middle' that benignly includes the 'margin' – truth and beauty can't be attained without using all the gifts God sends.

One feature of aspirational diversity is that by no means all of the staff or volunteers share an interest in Christianity. The community is enriched by people from a wide variety of religious and secular commitments.

2 Being a social enterprise keeps the institution close to the uncompromising realities of the economic climate, geopolitical tensions and tough commercial choices. St Martin's is exposed to major public events and trends. It has members of staff from 25 countries, and is thus closely affected by Brexit and changes in migration patterns. It relies on income from tourists and other visitors, and has thus experienced downturns triggered by terrorist incidents in central London. Meanwhile, it has to make judgements about what it means for its business to be an exemplary organization when the wider institution depends for its survival on the profits it makes. Moving to the London Living Wage was costly but unquestionably the right thing to do: working out a wise and just level of sick pay is a more complex exercise.

3 Working with homeless, destitute and vulnerably housed people brings to the institution a host of stories, some

troubling, some infuriating, some salutary, some enlightening, about the underside of life in London today and how people from different backgrounds come to find themselves there. It provides constant insight into human fragility, the flaws in welfare schemes, the resilience of those who have undergone arduous journeys, the suffering of those who prefer the unforgiving streets of London to the hardships of where they've migrated from, the survival instinct, self-destructive cycles, and the human cost of global change. Half the clientele come from beyond the UK, including a quarter from beyond the EU.

The greatest insight from this work is that the goal of social engagement is to achieve 'with' rather than to settle for 'for'.[8] That's to say, the work is about building on the assets of the person in question, balancing encouragement and challenge – rather than concentrating on their deficits and providing resources and information. You can't change people's lives – you can only walk alongside them while they find confidence and aptitude to address their trials themselves.

4 A cultural programme, in this case music and visual arts, both reflects and shapes the wider culture. At St Martin's, the arts are a medium of worship, a form of training, an expression of feeling, a means of generating income, a mode of teamwork and a celebration of being alive. The music programme strives to be at the same time (a) *aspirational*, with outstanding professional singers and emerging choral scholars, (b) *participatory*, with plenty of opportunity for those who are willing and able to learn, and (c) *financially sustainable*, with the income-generating parts broadly covering the costs of those aspects that are supported for their own sake.

The cultural programme is vital because it is the most accessible way in which the institution displays and celebrates the joys of life – rather than simply alleviating life's burdens. Purpose can never be simply about making the bad less bad; it must equally be about portraying and discovering what good looks like.

Fundamentally, St Martin's believes that the future is bigger than the past. Recent political movements have demonstrated that when people lose sight of a genuine telos, and lose confidence in their own ability to play a constructive role in advancing towards it, they resort to imagining a better past and seeking others to blame for inhibiting their ability to recreate it. At a place like St Martin's, people of immensely diverse social classes, racial backgrounds and experiences of flourishing and hardship cross paths, find common ground and are enhanced by encounter. This is what human flourishing and social cohesion look like. The challenge is to study its lessons, replicate it as appropriate and stimulate other communities to develop such institutions in their own context. That is in great part what this book is about.

HeartEdge

> It is too light a thing that you should be my servant
>> to raise up the tribes of Jacob
>> and to restore the survivors of Israel;
> I will give you as a light to the nations,
>> that my salvation may reach to the end of the earth.
>
> (Isaiah 49.6)

In many ways St Martin-in-the-Fields would like to be a 'normal' church, focused on congregational life, the cycle of the church year and being a good neighbour. But the account I have given above shows why its location and history mean that it is far from being a normal church. The movement that was created to turn the blessings of St Martin's into blessings for church and society more broadly is called HeartEdge – the name deriving from the vision statement explored above.

HeartEdge arose because significant numbers of delegations from the UK and overseas were coming to St Martin's to learn about the features of its life that are transferable and seeking to adapt and replicate them in their own contexts. This recognition of its national and international vocation led St Martin's in

February 2017 to launch HeartEdge, a national movement that now has ecumenical and international dimensions. It seeks the renewal of the church by catalysing kingdom communities. It aims to foster, not to impose; it sees the kingdom as God's gift to renew the church, rather than as a mission field to be conformed to the church's image; and it sees churches as lively and dynamic communities, rather than defensive and narrow congregations. Through HeartEdge, communities mentor one another, offer consultancy days to one another, and meet in larger gatherings to exchange ideas, encouragement and challenge. It seeks not to create clones of St Martin's, but to become the national embodiment of those committed to the vision to be 'At the heart. On the edge'.

Just as St Martin's aspires to be a community of hope, reimagining church and society through commerce, culture, compassion and congregational life, so HeartEdge cultivates an understanding of mission based around these 4 Cs. What's unique about St Martin's is not that it is engaged in commerce, culture, compassion or congregational life – many churches are, to different degrees – but that it's hugely invested in all four at the same time. HeartEdge rests on the conviction that the interplay of two, or preferably three or four, of these can profoundly enrich a church and can cross-fertilize one another to great effect. The movement is largely about encouraging and enabling churches to see such interplays begin, flourish and grow. This is what it means by describing itself as a national movement of kingdom churches: churches that believe the Holy Spirit is moving beyond the conventional notion of church, and believe in modelling the life of heaven by being open to partnership with what the Spirit is doing in the world.

The convictions of kingdom communities

I am aware that when a church gains a reputation for drawing attention to a 'social' or 'justice' agenda, and especially when it seeks to stand alongside excluded groups and when it points out inconsistencies in key doctrines, people may grow anxious that it has detached from its moorings in the Christian tradition. So I include in this introduction a more explicit account of the theological foundations of what I am calling kingdom communities.

Kingdom communities believe that Jesus' life offers us a template to talk about our lives, about the church and about the world – or, to use the jargon, discipleship, ministry and mission. The four key convictions of kingdom communities arise out of the template of Jesus' life. I call those four key convictions Christmas, Good Friday, Easter and Pentecost.

Christmas proclaims that every good thing of God and creation can be embodied in just one single life. God is infinite spirit: but the whole wonder of God can be communicated in one mortal, finite, material body. The incarnation makes clear that human flesh can convey ultimate truth; it can express not just fallibility and limitation but glory and grace. The parable speaks of one slave who buried his talent in the hillside and two that took theirs to market to face the risk of encounter. God is that slave who took the talent of creative love to the hurly-burly of creation rather than bury it in the safe hillside of sequestered eternity. We look on our human form and see its weakness and its folly; the Holy Spirit looks on our human form and makes it capable of opening a window on to heaven and a vision into the heart of God. Sin isn't 'living it up', existing too much; on the contrary, sin is failing to live to the full, refraining from embracing life in all its extent, focusing one's desires and energies on something less than, and unworthy of, the kingdom. Christmas tells us we meet God not by withdrawing from life but by immersing ourselves in it.

We lament the scarcity of God, assuming God should be everywhere and always; but Christmas shows us the abundance of God, the fullness of whom was pleased to dwell there and then. Through Christmas we learn not to search for mammon, the things that run out – comparison and competition, and their children, envy and greed – but to love the things that God gives in plenty, that never run short – love, joy, peace. God is plenty. Joy is to find and be overwhelmed by the abundance of

God. Sin is the fear that we won't have enough and the vain search to find security elsewhere.

Good Friday proclaims that there's no limit to which God will not go to be with us – indeed, that to be with us for ever Jesus will not only yield up his life but will even temporarily jeopardize his being with the Father. But Good Friday also embodies a paradox: that at humanity's lowest moment, at God's most horrifying moment, humanity is the closest it could ever be to God. This is the image that epitomizes the Christian faith: the naked, exposed, forsaken Jesus, the unmistakeable manifestation of our inseparability from God. In this is love, not that God conquers, not that we excel, but that when we disclose our very worst, God does not let us go. This expresses a strand of biblical faith that goes back to Judah's exile in Babylon. Deprived of land, king and temple, Judah yet discovers that it is closer to God than ever it was in the Promised Land. 'If I love thee for hope of heaven, then deny me heaven; if I love thee for fear of hell, then give me hell; but if I love thee for thyself alone, then give me thyself alone.' Judah had previously loved God for the hope of heaven or the fear of hell: now Judah says, 'Give me yourself alone' – and God replies, 'Here is myself alone.'

This reveals the conviction that there's a window into the heart of God that can be seen by those who experience adversity but is invisible to the comfortable. Which transforms mission. Mission is no longer the wise trying to make the foolish less foolish or the comfortable trying to make the distressed more comfortable. Now it is discipleship, because it is people recognizing that, if they are not being themselves oppressed, the chances are they are unconsciously implicated in or at least beneficiaries of the process of oppressing, and they must choose whose side to be on. And it's ministry, because it's the church perceiving that if it's to see God truly, it must be beside those who see God best, which is those who are on the cross or in exile. Which is why inclusion is such a problematic word. Inclusion is a word the comfortable use to say, 'We are a bunch of people in the centre whose lives are normal and sorted and privileged, and we really ought to open the doors and welcome people in and be a bit more thoughtful and kind and generous.' That makes inclusion a patronizing and paternalistic model. It assumes a centre and a periphery, where the centre gives kindly hospitality to the periphery, so the periphery feels humiliated and the centre feels smug. The comfortable need the oppressed more than the oppressed need the comfortable. If the comfortable experience their life as scarcity, it's most likely because they've closed their eyes to the gifts God is giving them in those they choose to regard as other.

The right questions are, 'If I'm oppressed, am I allowing myself to see God with clarity and humanity with mercy? If I'm not oppressed, is it because I'm complicit in perpetrating or overlooking oppression, and if I stopped being so wouldn't I quickly find myself oppressed too? And even if I'm not so colluding, if I want to see God, don't I know where God has promised most explicitly to be made known, in the lives of those who are oppressed? So isn't it time I hung out there, not assuming my role is to transform those lives, but first and most importantly to learn from them and see the world and God through their eyes?'

Easter offers a definition and redefinition of past and future. Human existence is experienced as a prison because of our panic about the past and the fear of the future. There's no genuine living in the present tense because our lives are dominated by bitterness and grief and humiliation about the past, and paralysed by anxiety and terror and horror about the future. Easter proclaims two central convictions: one about sin, and one about death; one about the past, and one about the future. The first is about the past. It's the forgiveness of sins. Forgiveness doesn't change the past. But it releases us from the power of the past. Forgiveness doesn't rewrite history. But it prevents our histories asphyxiating us. Forgiveness transforms our past from an enemy to a friend, from a horror-show of shame to a storehouse of wisdom. In the absence of forgiveness, we're isolated from our past, pitifully trying to bury or deny or forget or destroy the many things that haunt and overshadow and plague and torment us. Forgiveness doesn't change these things: but it does change their relationship to us. No longer do they imprison us or pursue us or surround us or stalk us. Now they accompany us, deepen us, teach us, train us. No longer do we hate them or curse them or resent them or begrudge them. Now we find acceptance, understanding, enrichment, even gratitude for them. That's the work of forgiveness. It's about the transformation of the prison of the past.

And the second Easter conviction is about the future. The life everlasting. Everlasting life doesn't take away the unknown element of the future: but it takes away the paroxysm of fear that engulfs the cloud of unknowing. Everlasting life doesn't dismantle the reality of death, the crucible of suffering, the agony of bereavement: but it offers life beyond death, comfort beyond suffering, companionship beyond separation. In the absence of everlasting life, we're terrified of our future, perpetually trying to secure permanence in the face of transitoriness, meaning in the face of waste, distraction in the face of despair. Everlasting life doesn't undermine human endeavour, but it rids it of the last word; evil is real, but it won't have the final say; death is coming, but it doesn't obliterate the power of God; identity is fragile, but that in us that resides in God will be changed into glory. Easter says there is forgiveness – so the past is a gift; and there is everlasting life – the future's our friend. That's what freedom means. We can truly exist. That's the gospel.

Pentecost proclaims that the work of reconciliation was not only the work of Jesus, incarnate among us, but is the central work of the church in ministry and mission. The church has no deeper work than reconciliation: its work is to reconcile people to God, to creation, to one another and to themselves. Every calling of ministry and mission is but an element of reconciliation, which involves telling a truthful story, proceeds through apology, penance and repentance, and issues in forgiveness, reconciliation, healing and resurrection. Justice isn't a virtue in itself – neither is truth, or even mercy: each finds its true meaning as a step on the way to reconciliation. When we weary of the ministry of reconciliation, exasperated that it's slow, or embarrassed that it's necessary, all we do is turn our hand to a more pliable or plausible context for reconciliation. There isn't anything else.

Baptism is the embodiment of reconciliation with God; the Eucharist is a paradigm of how reconciliation with God creates and makes possible a reconciled community. The term we use for instances of reconciliation, or steps on the way, or changed hearts, healed minds, energized bodies, renewed spirits, released souls that sketch the penumbra of reconciled feelings, words, gestures and action – that term is Holy Spirit. The Holy Spirit is the action of God that makes present today the reconciliation Jesus enacted once and for all. Sometimes that's through the ministry of the church; sometimes it's in the world in spite of the church; sometimes the church finds the humility to enjoy the reconciliation the Holy Spirit brings about in the world without the church's fingerprints getting on it.

Christmas, Good Friday, Easter and Pentecost name the four key convictions of kingdom communities. But we could call them abundance, grace, freedom and reconciliation.

The shape of this book

The book came into being as a result of being asked to give the Chalmers Lectures in Edinburgh in 2019, and I have sought to preserve the integrity of the six lectures by making them the substance of the six chapters presented here. Other material that I regard as helpful for giving context and explanation for the lectures I have provided in this introduction and in the appendix.

The opening chapter sets the global social and economic context in which I believe institutions like St Martin-in-the-Fields are timely and significant, because they cultivate the ordinary virtues and encourage dynamic forms of belonging and blessing. In this first chapter I set out what I call the seven characteristics of kingdom churches, to make explicit the ways

HeartEdge – the renewal movement initiated by St Martin-in-the-Fields – is an idea for our time.

The second chapter identifies money as a key for eliciting what lifestyle many churches suppose the gospel requires and thus for what those churches think they are doing. I consider how the Reformation altered the church's attitude to money and to discipleship. I go on to propose a further reform in how churches may relate to money that keeps their mission broad.

The final four chapters follow the 4 Cs of HeartEdge, considering in turn commerce, compassion, culture and congregation. In Chapter 3 I offer three models for how a congregation may engage in commercial activity and review the strengths and weaknesses of each. I explore misgivings about such endeavours and seek to articulate what appropriate practice might involve. In Chapter 4 I go back a hundred years to consider a critique of conventional charity, and go on to suggest key criteria for assessing whether compassionate mission undertaken by congregations is healthy and helpful.

Chapter 5 begins on a broader canvas and charts what we mean by culture and why the church is particularly well positioned to engage and promote it. I establish some proposals for how culture can advance a congregation's mission and conclude with a humble example of how this has proved to be fruitful in one context. Finally, in Chapter 6 I revisit the seven characteristics of kingdom churches and scrutinize each one for how it genuinely enriches congregational life, without ever losing sight of a larger context of the church's witness on a political, social and economic plane.

The book concludes with an appendix that seeks to offer ways to evaluate how well a congregation is doing that go beyond conventional metrics of headcount and balance sheet. This is not designed as a capitulation to commodifying tendencies in the church – quite the opposite: it is created precisely to give those who wish to advance a broader understanding of church and mission some way of evaluating for themselves and demonstrating to others the true quality of what they are trying to do.

Notes

1 Of course, it's not really new. Origen was musing over the possibility of universal salvation as early as the third century.

2 I first heard this prayer spoken by Michael Nazir-Ali, to whom I remain indebted. After 25 years of searching for its source, Georgie Illingworth, to whom I am most grateful, directed my attention to the work of the mystic Rabi'a. Jane Hirshfield's translation of Rabi'a's original prayer goes as follows: 'O my Lord, if I worship you from fear of hell, burn me in hell. If I worship you from hope of Paradise, bar me from its gates. But if I worship you for yourself alone, grant me then the beauty of your Face.' See www.poetryfoundation.org/poems/55267/o-my-lord-56d236a947ec8, and Jane Hirshfield, ed., *Women in Praise of the Sacred: 43 Centuries of Spiritual Poetry by Women* (New York: HarperCollins, 1994). I can't recall whether my translation is the work of Michael Nazir-Ali or my own flawed memory, but I'm now so attached to the version with which I'm familiar that I'm recording it thus rather than in Jane Hirshfield's translation.

3 This is the argument of Samuel Wells with David Barclay and Russell Rook, *For Good: The Church and the Future of Welfare* (Norwich: Canterbury Press, 2017).

4 Roger L. Martin and Sally R. Osberg, *Getting Beyond Better: How Social Entrepreneurship Works* (Boston, MA: Harvard Business Review Press, 2015), pp. 7–11.

5 L. Gregory Jones, *Christian Social Innovation: Renewing Wesleyan Witness* (Nashville: Abingdon, 2016), p. 5.

6 The original sermon is in Samuel Wells, *Speaking the Truth: Preaching in a Pluralistic Culture* (Nashville: Abingdon, 2008), pp. 167–72.

7 Wendell Berry, 'Two Economies', *Review and Expositor* 81 (2) (1984) pp. 209–23.

8 For more on the difference, see my *Incarnational Mission: Being with the World* (Grand Rapids and Norwich: Eerdmans and Canterbury Press, 2018), *Incarnational Ministry: Being with the Church* (Grand Rapids and Norwich: Eerdmans and Canterbury Press, 2017), and *A Nazareth Manifesto: Being with God* (Oxford: Wiley-Blackwell, 2015).

I

For Such a Time as This:
The Church's Opportunity

I don't regard Christianity as a religion, if by 'religion' we mean a genus that sits among other religions, which share a concern with spirituality and often life beyond death, are preoccupied with holy figures and sacred rituals, and tend to be associated by others with conservative attitudes and a sense of superiority and judgement over the mass of earthly humanity. Instead, I regard Christianity as alternative society. Alternative in terms of time, because it believes God's future, which we may call the kingdom, is already overlapping with our present; and alternative in terms of space, because while tending to itself in ministry, the church is always sharing space with the world in mission. But alternative most of all in terms of story; Christian identity is not a possession to be owned or an achievement to be cherished or even a quality to be realized – it is a gift to be received. That gift comes in two main forms: it's the gift of a new past, in which the mistakes we have perpetrated are healed and the damage we have undergone is redeemed, collectively known as forgiveness; and the gift of a new future, in which the dread of punishment is lifted and the fear of oblivion is disarmed. Thus Christianity is a new present, a true gift, a way of life made possible by Easter and Pentecost, an anticipation of eternal life with God.

Likewise, I don't regard Christianity in the United Kingdom as being uniquely in peril. It is true that the time when Christianity and citizenship were virtually synonymous has long gone, that regular church attendance is much less common, that marks of affiliation, notably baptism, are less the norm, and that recourse to clergy in times of life transition, especially funerals and weddings, is less prevalent. But the church has faced challenges in every generation. Dr Arnold, Headmaster of Rugby, in a letter to a member of SPCK, wrote, 'The Church as it now stands no human power can save.'[1] That was in 1832. There was no time when the church in the United Kingdom 'got it right'. There is no challenge today that is different in kind from what has gone before. At the same time there is no complacency in the kingdom of God.

My task in this book is to recognize, in the words of Chesterton, that 'The Christian ideal has not been tried and found wanting. It has been found difficult; and left untried.'[2] Thus undaunted and even emboldened by the cries of peril, my task is to articulate and envision Christianity as an alternative society in terms appropriate for contemporary conditions and circumstances. I'm not suggesting no one has been a real Christian before now: more that there are dimensions of church life, notably its understanding of the kingdom, that have been long neglected or regarded as a minority pursuit, yet are the key to renewal. In this opening chapter I seek to locate the UK church in a global and gospel story, and thereby identify the particular opportunity Christianity has at such a time as this. In the subsequent chapters I direct attention to how it may take advantage of such an opportunity.

I want to relate three overlapping but distinct stories of where the world is at present, before seeing what might be the church's opportunity at such a time as this.

Lament for the casualties of liberalism

I'm going to call the first story 'casualties of liberalism'. This is what we could call the failure of the success of the liberal project. I want to explore a book that constitutes a lament for what our society has lost that it has no prospect of replacing.

In their book *The Politics of Virtue: Post-liberalism and the Human Future*,[3] theologian John Milbank and political scientist

Adrian Pabst offer a prophetic elucidation of a crisis that Brexit and Trump have so vividly epitomized. Democracy has yielded oligarchies and the tyranny of majorities; capitalism has been criminalized and become venal; there's a pervasive sense of a society that's losing the adhesive qualities that held it together. Milbank and Pabst, never short of a grand phrase, call this the 'metacrisis of liberalism'. They position liberalism as an ethos that philosophically 'refuses to accept anything not rationally proven or demonstrable' and 'disallows any public influence for the non-proven – the emotively or faithfully affirmed'.[4] Liberalism believes we are 'isolated, autonomous individuals whose activities can only be coordinated by an absolutely sovereign centre, holding a monopoly of violence, power and ultimate decision making'.[5] It has economic and political manifestations, contrasting the free market with the bureaucratic state, after the fashion of Reagan and Thatcher, yet also social and cultural dimensions, insisting on individual rights and equality of opportunity for self-expression[6] – but, crucially, liberalism regards the economic and political as prior to social bonds and cultural ties, making the latter subject to law and contract.[7]

Sociologically, liberalism became normative from the 1950s: 'after that decade, the whole of social reality, including the family, became gradually capitalized and commodified, through the construction of "the consumer" rather than "the worker" as the crucial economic and cultural actor.'[8] Theologically, liberalism arose in the seventeenth century, when agreement concerning the transcendent good began to be associated with conflict and warfare: Christianity believes in an original peace, disrupted by sin, whereas liberalism assumes an original agonistic condition, which only contract and the state can restrain. Biologically, liberalism perceives a meaningless 'nature', and a non-existent 'spirit', and thus reduces reality to the establishment of power through beneficial exchange conducted by a technologically assisted abstract human will in a world without intrinsic meaning.[9]

Liberalism isn't simply a boo-word: the authors acknowledge that there is a generous sense of the term, denoting the

33

upholding of constitutional liberties to ensure the exercise of justice, the humanitarian treatment of the weak and the creative flourishing of all. But lurking amid the benign aspirations of equality, freedom and happiness, they sniff the assumption that we are basically 'self-interested, fearful, greedy and egotistic creatures, unable to see beyond our own selfish needs and, therefore, prone to violent conflict'.[10] The authors match each chapter of their diagnosis of the crisis of liberalism with a corresponding account of a cure. That cure is, in a word, virtue.

Virtue is the recovery of the notion of telos, a final purpose towards which all activity is oriented. Milbank and Pabst explain virtue in this way:

A more universal flourishing for all can be obtained when we continuously seek to define the goals of human society as a whole and then to discern the variously different . . . roles that are required for the mutual advancement of those shared aims.[11]

What this is describing, I suspect, is the same thing people recall as the goodness that was at large when Britain was at war in 1916 or 1940: a common project – a team game. The aim of social relating is not 'mainly the satisfaction of private predilections, but relationship as such, and the good of the other, besides oneself, in the widest possible range'.[12] Meaning belongs primarily in the social, the relational – the specifically located.

In a phrase after my own heart, Milbank and Pabst say, 'Community is always a "being with" . . . a series of exchanged and binding gifts, which originally constitute society prior to any economic or political contract.'[13] To pursue such foundational relationality is to become vulnerable to wounds inflicted by the other. The market and the state promise to insulate us from such hurt through impersonal transactions; but in bureaucratizing security we lose the capacity for genuine joy. Freedom is not a given but a gift that can be discovered by all through healthy formation.[14] In practice, virtue translates into fostering intermediate associations such as manufacturing and trading guilds, cooperatives, ethical and profit-sharing businesses, trade unions, voluntary organizations, universities and free cities. Following the Italian thinkers Bruni and Zamagni, and in the tradition of writers such as Maurice Glasman, Milbank and Pabst outline a whole vision of a civil economy to amplify the economics of virtue.

In a judgement that puts its finger on concerns central to my argument in this book, Milbank and Pabst identify the connection between their argument and contemporary preoccupations:

> Increasingly liberal-democratic politics revolves around a supposed guarding against alien elements: the terrorist, the refugee, the foreigner, the criminal, the dissident, the welfare-scrounger, the shirker, the spendthrift, the non-'hard-working family,' and those deemed deficient in 'entrepreneurship.' Populism seems more and more to be an inevitable, if ironic, consequence of liberal emptiness of purpose and its founding assumption of a reactive warding off of violence and evil.[15]

The book is a cry to recognize the procedural follies and criminal economics that have undermined the social and cultural relatedness and embeddedness that constitute the true goods of human existence. We have, as a liberal-democratic society, lost the plot. The plot is and should always have been about healthy, gifted forms of relationship and the cultivation of creative expression in the service of the common good. Who could be against that? It turns out, our whole political and economic superstructure.

Hope in ordinary virtue

If John Milbank and Adrian Pabst leave us with a sombre mood of lament, a second, overlapping, recent study offers a humble but plausible source of hope.

In *The Ordinary Virtues: Moral Order in a Divided World*,[16] Canadian professor, broadcaster and politician Michael Ignatieff asks the question, 'Is globalization drawing us together morally?' He seeks to answer that question as he embarks on a seven-stop world tour. The answer, it turns out, is no. Everywhere, the secular narratives that make sense of public life – the inevitability of technical progress, the spread of democracy, the triumph of liberalism – are in crisis.[17] Democratic sovereignty and universalist rights are on a collision course across the globe, and the biggest flashpoint is the tension between migrants and local culture. Grand empires have been replaced not by universal principles but by an assertion of individual entitlements unmatched by corresponding duties. People judge behaviour not by a universal code but instead want 'to think well of ourselves and at the very least to ensure that others don't think too badly'.[18] But beyond that, what shapes people's lives? Ignatieff argues it's a desire for moral order – 'a framework of expectations that allow them to think of their life, no matter how brutal or difficult, as meaningful'.[19] Moral values are not converging. We live in competing local and global worlds. Yet we face the same challenges: how much to trust those who rule us, tolerate those who are different, forgive those who have wronged us, and rebuild life when its fruits have been swept away.

Ignatieff points out two rival perspectives on the imperial era, running from 1490 to 1970. In the first, Christianity, commerce and civilization, epitomized in imperial administration, united humankind in a story of technological and moral progress. In the other, the unifying global cash nexus crushed the local, the traditional, the vernacular in favour of wage labour and colonial domination. But now we face something new, and different: a post-imperial era. For the first time since 1490, no power dominates the global economy. Russia and China have joined the party. But, as Ignatieff points out, 'The antiglobal counter-revolution comes from political forces on the left who mobilize in opposition to the ecological destruction and distributive inequality of global capitalism, and it comes from the right from those who believe capitalism destroys traditions, national identities, and sovereignty.'[20]

The most striking expression of this counter-revolution was the 2016 American election, in which millions of ordinary voters 'made plain that they feel they are the victims of globalization, not its beneficiaries'.[21] People everywhere are 'struggling to make sense of convulsive, destabilizing change'.[22] Narratives such as the inevitability of technological progress, the spread of democracy and the triumph of scientific rationality founder on the rocks of unexpected events. Everywhere people are seeking with one hand to benefit from globalization, yet with the other hand struggling to retain their jobs, communities and settled values.

Ignatieff is an acute observer of the competition to fill the space left behind by the globalization of empire. One key driver is new technology, which brings rich and poor face to face, generating envy, resentment, ambition, while triggering migration from poor countries and discontent within rich countries about inequalities that used to be invisible. The result is a rhetoric that everyone has an equal right to speak and be heard, alongside a reality that some voices are heard more than others. But a consistent feature is the diminishment of priestly or political authority in telling people what to think. Morality is not about obedience, but about 'affirming the self and the moral community to which one belongs'. Individuals across the globe almost universally regard moral choice as their own responsibility.[23] Another driver is the emergence of two entrepreneurs of moral globalization: on one side, executives of multinational corporations, who set the rates of exchange that bind developing world producers with first-world consumers; on the other side, the activists and NGOs that have replaced the colonial administrator as the bearer of universal values, advocating for ethical sourcing of commodities and making anticorruption a new norm. While some castigate the powerful, others fear that no one is really in charge, and war, migration, inequality, poverty and ecological fragmentation will increasingly stalk the earth.

Ignatieff's proposal in the face of these challenges is ordinary virtue. Trust, honesty, politeness, forbearance and respect are, he says, the 'operating system of any community'.[24] He finds tolerance, forgiveness, reconciliation and resilience (a blend of buoyancy, elasticity and improvisation) to be life skills acquired through experience rather than through moral judgement or deliberative thought. In a paragraph that is surely a gesture to St Paul's hymn to love, he explains, lyrically:

> Ordinary virtue does not generalize. It does not forget or ignore difference; does not pay much attention to the human beneath our diversity; is not much interested in ethical consistency; works to live and let live as an organizing assumption in dealings with others, but retreats to loyalty towards one's own when threatened; is anti-ideological and anti-political; favours family and friends over strangers and other citizens; is hopeful about life without much of a metaphysics of the future and is often surprised by its own resilience in the face of adversity; believes, finally, that ethics is not an abstraction but just what you do and how you live, and that displaying the virtues, as best you can, is the point and purpose of a human life.[25]

More simply, ordinary virtue is a struggle with the ordinary vices of greed, lust, envy and hatred. In the face of extraordinary vice, such as terrorism, it can crumble; but when the crisis passes, ordinary virtues rebuild through networks of trust and resilience. This is a vision in some tension with a Christian ethic, and for the most part a pale shadow of what 1 Corinthians 13 is calling us to: but it's a significant appeal for a ground-up, pragmatic, applicable baseline for human coexistence.

Becoming more human

Located somewhere between the first, economic and philosophical, analysis and the second, social and ethical, one is a narrative that comes from a combination of thinkers close to the G20 process in a series of contributions to the *Global Solutions Journal*. Their contention is that social and economic progress, which had marched in step for 30 years after 1945, became decoupled after 1980, triggering the signs of global distress seen today. Colm Kelly and Blair Sheppard, senior consultants for PwC (PricewaterhouseCoopers, a multinational professional services network), identify three positive forces that benefitted the world for a generation or two, but are now mistrusted.[26] First, *globalization* started with worldwide economic institutions, and came to involve the migration of people, goods, capital and information, thereby boosting trade. Second, *technology* embraced transport, the internet, biotech, healthcare, and now artificial intelligence. And third, *financialization* narrowed metrics of progress down to GDP and shareholder value, reversing the trend since the 1930s by which companies understood their role as to work for the common good. Together these three phenomena lifted billions out of poverty and raised the global quality of life immeasurably.

The major changes were the universal adoption of market economics after 1989, the emergence of the internet, and the cascade of financial deregulation, all leading to the shift of first products and subsequently services towards countries with large populations and low wage rates. Economic indicators continued to rise, but social indicators started to fall seriously behind. While the richest and poorest benefitted greatly, a whole swathe of the population in the developed world made little or no gains in the 20 years prior to the 2008 crash. Many people sense a diminishing control over their destiny and an attenuation of their social ties. The result has been the erosion of trust in mainstream institutions – government, business, media, education and NGOs. In addition, economic growth has failed to respect its wider ecology, hastening 'climate change, ocean acidification, depletion of vital natural resources, desertification, falling water tables, overfishing, deforestation, and biodiversity loss'.[27]

A realignment of globalization, technology and financialization is critical. Kelly and Sheppard point out that an economy is 'a dynamic and evolving framework of rules, habits, agreements, behaviours, and practices that facilitates meeting the needs of people and their communities, and engages human skill and effort, and well as technology and capital, to do so'.[28] Thus the current economy needs to be refreshed with a broader vision. Healthy communities, smart cities and transferable skills are among those metrics that go broader than the narrow measures of success that have been exposed over the last decade.

The economist Denis Snower builds on this work to point out that 'the world's produced goods and services are growing at the expense of its social and environmental capital' – what he calls a 'dangerous decoupling'.[29] He summarizes the situation like this:

> Economically, the problem manifests itself through rising inequalities. Socially, it comes as a crisis of identities, arising from two by-products of globalization: growing interactions with strangers (due to personal mobility and international competition for jobs) and the weakening of local social ties (due to the rise of global production, distribution and marketing networks and the fall in location-specific job security). Psychologically, the problem often takes the form of a perceived loss of life meaning.
>
> The resulting dissatisfaction of the relatively vulnerable social groups has generated rising nationalism, populism and cross-cultural intolerance in many countries, along with a falling appreciation of the benefits of democracy. This problem threatens to stoke social conflicts and undermine the legitimacy of the political and economic systems responsible for the rising worldwide material wealth, while simultaneously depleting more of our natural and social capital.[30]

Put another way, the emphasis on economics has delivered greater average wealth, but has failed to deliver three important outcomes: equality, empowerment and solidarity. People in general do not feel greater motivation, capacity or opportunity; they do not sense a growth in care, belonging, meaning, identity or trust.[31] They feel an increasing sense of powerlessness and isolation.

Snower identifies five turning points across 250 years. The first industrial revolution created steam and machine power. The second industrial revolution created electricity, cars and planes. Wealth moved to the developed world, artisans gave way to factory workers, work left the home. Huge dislocation was partly addressed by the emergence of the welfare state. From 1980 there followed three digital revolutions. The first shifted production to the six emerging countries, China, India, Indonesia, Korea, Poland and Thailand; national boundaries became less significant, and skilled labour became paramount. The second involved artificial intelligence, robotics and cloud computing. This was the one that severely hit the middle-income groups. The strategy of skilling one's way to job security and prosperity through knowledge and technical competence no longer works. A worker or machine elsewhere in the world can snatch that job away in a second. The third, almost upon us, will see robots taking over not only manual labour but even sophisticated cognitive work, potentially transforming medical diagnosis and legal judgements. While the industrial revolutions transported goods and the digital revolutions transported ideas, this new phase is set to overcome the challenge of transporting people by transporting machines instead.

This starts to beg the question of what it means to be human. Since the Enlightenment the answer has been associated with such cognitive abilities as other animals lack; but now machines may share many such abilities. Snower maintains that human identity lies with cooperation and innovation. He maintains our social connections rest on our capacity for 'mentalizing (reading the thoughts of others), empathy (feeling the feelings of others), compassion (the desire to relieve the suffering of others), [and] loving-kindness (the desire to promote the happiness of others)'.[32] These capacities are about relationship and purpose. And here emerges the irony.

Since the Industrial Revolution, people have been required to become machine-like, in order to interact effectively with the machines that they had invented. When the machines did simple, repetitive tasks, the workers operating them needed to do simple, repetitive tasks as well. When the machines became more versatile and programmable, the workers were required to become more versatile, but only within the bounds of the existing programs. But in the Third Digital Revolution, people will be required to exercise their abilities for sociality and discovery that they have developed over tens of thousands of years. Humans, in short, will have the opportunity to become more human again.[33]

It's time to review these three stories of our global plight and opportunity. Milbank and Pabst, sensing the philosophical emptiness of liberalism, take confidence in the social, the relational, the specifically located – in a 'series of exchanged and binding gifts' that transcend any economic contract. Ignatieff, despite the fact that he upholds the philosophy of liberalism in contrast to Milbank and Pabst, still offers texture and global thick description of the virtue that Milbank and Pabst commend. He observes tolerance, forgiveness, reconciliation and resilience as building blocks of global coexistence, and maintains as widespread the conviction that 'displaying the virtues, as best you can, is the point and purpose of a human life'. Snower gives narrative and urgency to these convictions. He shows the class interest and global dynamic of social and economic change. But he offers a tantalizing prospect of an imminent future that, while challenging, offers to bring humanity closer to its true identity.

In the second half of this chapter I want to reflect on these proposals in the light of rival visions of the future of the church.

Three stories of church

Charles Taylor's book *A Secular Age,* perhaps more than any other, has come to be regarded as a significant theoretical analysis of the social and religious changes most North Atlantic congregations are experiencing on a practical level. Taylor offers three understandings of secularity. The first is that religion has withdrawn (or been excluded) from public life; one can engage in politics or society and seldom if ever encounter significant declarations or rituals of belief; faith and aspiration of conformity to ultimate reality is now assumed to be a private matter. There is no civil ban on usury or insistence on orthodox conviction. The second is 'the falling off of religious belief and practice, in people turning away from God, and no longer going to Church'. The third is 'a move from a society where a belief in God is unchallenged and indeed, unproblematic, to one in which it is understood to be one option among others, and frequently not the easiest one to embrace'.[34]

Taylor conceives of Christianity not so much as a structure of belief but as lived experience. Thus he describes the real challenge to Christianity in the West today as a 'middle position' between a sense of God's grace and the misery of absence, despair or loss. This middle position is a routine order

> in which we are doing things which have some meaning for us; for instance, which contribute to our ordinary happiness, or which are fulfilling in various ways, or which contribute to what we conceive of as the good. Or often, in the best scenario, all three: for instance, we strive to live happily with spouse and children, while practising a vocation which we find fulfilling, and also which constitutes an obvious contribution to human welfare.[35]

If we accept Taylor's three kinds of secularity, and recognize that in the United Kingdom, in spite of some significant aspects of the visibility of Christianity in the public realm, the falling off of religious belief and practice is real, and the move to a general perception of Christianity as one option among others is undeniable; and if we are acquainted with what Taylor calls the middle condition, of domestic contentment, professional fulfilment, and an aspiration to benefit human welfare as the almost universal purpose of our age; what then is the strategy for the church? I suggest that the two strategies that are currently most prominent and vocal correspond to Taylor's two proposals. I believe what is required, in the light of the global stories described earlier, is a different approach.

The most strident strategy, in the present context, is to accept Taylor's portrayal of the middle position almost uncritically and to seek to instrumentalize or to adapt Christianity to make the church the ideal route to such a position, with the complement of an agreeable helping of grace and limit experiences. Christianity is attractive because the church is full of people who appear successfully to have attained the middle position, with happy families, healthy careers and commendable contributions to general welfare, either through or (perhaps more often) alongside their careers. In addition, Christianity offers a guide for self-discipline and a sympathetic body of wisdom on loving marriage, resilient child-rearing, suitable conduct in the workplace and worthy goals for public benefit. Moreover, a strong emphasis on personal religious experience yields expectation and fulfilment of the desire for intimate, passionate and memorable moments of encounter with transcendent relationship. And whether in a search for more potential converts, or as a result of surplus energy to enhance public welfare, social action projects often result, and these too can make the strategy more attractive, more wholesome and more visible.

When the production standards are high, and the routes towards achieving the middle position are smooth and effective, it might appear there's a lot to be said for this strategy. One of its most appealing features is that it's not seeking to restore some historic place of the church in society; it's not going against the grain of Taylor's secular analysis. It knows Christianity is one option among many: it simply seeks to make it the most compelling option for achieving life-goals that are seldom questioned. Of course, the main problem with it is its largely uncritical acceptance of the middle position as a worthy model of discipleship, and the bourgeois assumptions that tend to accompany such an acceptance. For those for whom a conventional nuclear household or a fulfilling career are unrealizable or undesirable, the appeal is less strong. It's a model that could prove deeply vulnerable to the kinds of social changes envisaged by the third digital revolution identified earlier; partly because it accepts that faith is a private matter and has no apparent political or social vision that challenges or affects the status quo. Deep down it's instrumentalizing Christianity for something that's a false idea which is in the end a contradiction of the gospel.

The alternative strategy in relation to Taylor's analysis is to focus less on the lived experience of faith and to be more exercised with Taylor's notions of secularity. This view invests a great deal in the constitutional privilege of the Church of England, the role of the monarch as head of the church and defender of the faith, the place of bishops as the 26 Lords Spiritual in the Upper House, the nearly 7,000 church schools, and the place of Christianity in national institutions such as the charter of the BBC; and thus appeals to some kind of guaranteed place of the church at the heart of the nation. It tends to focus on Christianity as a cultural phenomenon, and to invest much in somewhat sixteenth-century expectations of England, Britain or the United Kingdom as a Christian nation. This tends to be less a requirement that so-called Christian values should be instilled in citizens and expected to be upheld by residents than a highly sensitized concern for any encroachment on Christian liberties – for example the right of a nurse to wear a cross around her neck in a working environment. In less confrontational form it appears as a mood of lament that blends the three forms of secularity Taylor delineates, and blames them all on a real or imagined secularist agenda.

Part of the problem with this approach, which is upheld, to some degree, by many across the theological range, is that it is counterproductive. The more such things as constitutional privileges are claimed as a right and entitlement, the more they are jeopardized and appear problematic. To maintain, on the basis of historical memory and cultural inheritance, that the United Kingdom is a Christian nation is to imagine a rose-tinted fantasy of the past and transport it to a very different present. It is also to forget that, whether or not these privileges were good for the country, they were not always good for the church, because they taught the church to rely for its flourishing on entitlements rather than on God's grace and its own endeavour. The real issue, though, is the mood of beleaguered lament. This is a view that things are slipping away and we should hang on to them for as long as we can. It is not a vision of a future bigger than the past. And it is a view too easily hijacked and made part of a political agenda isolationist in ethos and hostile to diversity. It has nothing to offer the third digital revolution; it's arguable whether it ever adapted to the first industrial revolution. What it doesn't understand is the danger of turning Christianity and the church into another social/political interest group, obsessed by threats to its identity and territory, and constantly feeling imposed upon or marginalized. It forgets that the church needs to be a blessing to the culture and people of the country – or it has no right to be heard at all.

I believe a different approach from these two strategies is required. In relation to Taylor's analysis, it needs to accept the falling-off of religious belief and practice as a fact, but do so without particular lament, for it needs to be mindful that what often passed as belief and practice was not always a full expression of the extent and dimensions of the kingdom of God. It needs to recognize a culture in which Christianity is one option among others as a reality, and seek to incorporate Taylor's notion of faith as lived experience, rather than simply belief, as the ground on which dialogue now takes place. People disregard or dismiss Christianity less often because they conclude that Darwin disproved the Bible than because they have little or no exposure to how the church is a life-changing or existential blessing to people in crisis, trouble or distress. But a fresh approach needs to rise to the challenge of Taylor's first version of secularity: it must contest the easy concession that faith is a private matter, and insist (to itself more than to others) that faith must make a visible and practical difference not only in the habits of individuals but in the collective activity of associations and communities.

In short, Christianity must take this opportunity to be what it was always called to be: an alternative society, overlapping and sharing space with regular society, but living in a different time – that's to say, modelling God's future in our present. It's not enough to cherish the scriptures, embody the sacraments, set time aside for prayer, and shape disciples' character in the ways of truth, if such practices simply withdraw disciples for select periods, uncritically then to return them after a brief pause to a world struggling with inequality, identity and purpose. The church must also model what the kingdom of God (its term for the alternative society, its language of God's future now) means and entails in visible and tangible form. An act of God should not be an unfortunate and uninsurable random occurrence that derails a journey or destroys a house; it should be the daily miracle of a community that lives by faith and in whose life are seen the things God makes possible.

In keeping with Michael Ignatieff's prescription, what's needed are communities of ordinary virtues, but ones infused with grace: thus trust, honesty, politeness, forbearance and respect are the bedrock of such communities, while tolerance, forgiveness, reconciliation and resilience are among its abiding graces. But following Milbank and Pabst, these communities reject the 'guarding against alien elements' and the 'reactive warding off violence and evil'. These communities go beyond what Ignatieff found by seeing the stranger as God's gift. Meanwhile, unlike Ignatieff's ordinary virtue, these communities see the future as bigger than the past – because now is our salvation nearer than when we first believed; in other words, the kingdom is something God brings rather than something we achieve – a purpose rather than a goal. In accordance with Milbank and Pabst's vision, these communities believe a more universal flourishing for all can be obtained when we continuously seek to define the goals of human society as a whole and then discern the variously different roles that are required for the mutual advancement of those shared aims.

But crucially these communities have much to offer in relation to Snower's five-chapter story, when it comes to the challenges of the digital age, and the second and third digital revolutions. This is because they are precisely concerned with what makes us human. They are specifically devoted to demonstrate how, in Milbank and Pabst's language, the aim of social relating is not mainly the satisfaction of private predilections, but relationship as such, and the good of the other, besides oneself, in the widest possible range. For these communities, as for Milbank and Pabst, meaning belongs primarily in the social, the relational, the specifically located. Community is always a 'being with', a series of exchanged and binding gifts, which originally constitute society prior to any economic or political contract. In this sense these communities are less vulnerable to social and economic changes than a strategy that uncritically focuses on achieving Taylor's 'middle position', which rests on precisely the kind of fulfilling work the third digital revolution looks set to strip away.

Here is a sevenfold proposal for what such a reimagining of church and society might involve.

1 *In contrast to fear, recognizable communities of hope, embodying a liberating story of reconciliation and grace.*
However bland and appealing Taylor's middle position might seem, it masks at least three kinds of fear. Fear of death is the apprehension of something that is set to take away everything that a hard-working life has secured. Fear of the other or the stranger is a fear of spending unlimited time in the company of (or in conflict with) those whose goals are incompatible or in competition with one's own. Fear of loss of meaning is the sense that some of the things death will involve have already come about – for example, that one cannot positively influence the world for good. The Christian gospel of reconciliation is that God in Christ has redeemed past failures and losses, both damage inflicted and hurts received, making God saviour not judge and turning enemy into friend. The gospel of grace is that God in Christ has, through resurrection, turned the future from terrifying oblivion into everlasting gift. Communities of hope embody this liberation.

2 *In contrast to exclusion, distinctive congregations whose life is shaped and renewed through the energy and gifts of those culturally, economically and socially 'on the edge', and whose diversity reflects the diverse glory of God.*

If the church experiences its life as scarcity, and yet at the same time fails to recognize the gifts God is giving it for renewal through those whom church and society have historically excluded, then the church's scarcity is self-inflicted. The mind-set of inclusion is inadequate, because inclusion suggests an established and righteous middle that benevolently and mag-nanimously draws in a vulnerable or unfortunate fringe. Better is a recognition that the church is impoverished unless and until it cherishes at its heart those with whom Christ spent most of his ministry, and in whom the Spirit is most alive today. The bland mantra of diversity hides the theological truth that God is more diverse than creation: the kaleidoscope of the Trinity is more many-splendoured than the human imagination can comprehend or any community can resemble.

3 *In contrast to despair, faithful disciples who have discovered how God is made known in times of adversity and who thus walk with the dispossessed in order to be close to God.*

The Bible came into being in exile, when the people of God came to discover a deeper understanding of their Maker and Redeemer than they had ever found in the Promised Land. That understanding enabled the first disciples to realize God had been made known in Christ's crucifixion like never before. Henceforth, suffering and bewilderment are not simply to be regarded as causes of distress – still less as signs of punishment – but as potential moments of transfiguration when God's being and companionship is made known in a new way. God is not an instrument to use to solve problems or gain security, but a mystery to be entered and in so doing to find true life.

4 *In contrast to decline, humble institutions whose need for financial sustainability opens their lives to the skill, vision and wisdom of those who scarcely or only partly share their faith.*

Churches have not always been a blessing to their neighbourhoods, but when they have been, they have often found it difficult to sustain their life financially. Just as congregational stewardship binds a local church by naming needs that bring forth gifts, so the practice of commercial enterprise is an incarnate form in which a congregation may both offer and receive from its surrounding community. And if it can do so according to exemplary business practices, it can broaden its witness of what the kingdom looks like. Thus it breaks the myth of the 'middle position', secure in its self-sufficiency, and draws out energies and talents others are eager to give and the church is blessed to receive.

5 *In contrast to defensiveness, fertile centres of creative and artistic flourishing through which people apprehend beauty in the world and talent in themselves and one another.*
Being alive is a mystery it takes more than a lifetime to comprehend; being fully alive is the aspiration of all who follow the one who came that all who live may live life to the full. As God the Father is creator, and that creation involves passion in the Son and empowerment in the Spirit, so creativity, passion and empowerment must be part of what it means to reflect the image of God. The imitation of Christ means not awed obedience, but living as Christ lived, igniting energies and talents and gifts and joys, in performance and visual arts, wherever people find inspiration and discover hope. No one knows better than the creative artist the risk of trusting that God will provide.

6 *In contrast to denial, penitent communities that recognize the individual and corporate legacy of the misuse of power and the dominance of some social groups over others, nationally and internationally, and are seeking new forms of practice and relationship.*
The church is a learning community, always open to discovery, new recognition, greater truth, transformed perspectives and wider vision. This means a continual practice of repentance,

over what was once thought good, permissible, of no account, deniable, and now comes explicitly to be rendered shameful, demeaning, exclusionary, wrong. If the church, by more legitimate means than often hitherto, is once again to become respected, authoritative and honoured, it must not make the mistakes that went before – or must, at least, strive with all integrity not to. The church has no monopoly on right action – indeed it might have more temptation to self-deception than many. The gospel is founded on forgiveness, not sinlessness, and the path to forgiveness is sometimes slow and painful.

7 *In contrast to turning inwards, thriving churches that individually and corporately are seen as an unqualified blessing by their neighbourhoods and nation.*

God's original call to Abraham was to be a blessing to the nations. It is perhaps the saddest fact about the church of our times that an institution that was once regarded as harmless and out of touch is now widely perceived, especially by the young, to be positively against what they take to be the universally acknowledged good of live and let live. It used to be a cliché to recall that William Temple named the church the one institution that exists for those outside it; but it's an out-of-fashion cliché that could do with being well known again. Being a blessing seldom means having all the answers and channelling all the resources: it means being one around whom others come alive, find their voice, feel accepted, gain confidence, can find trust and love and hope. It doesn't sound like much. But it's almost a forgotten art.

Conclusion

I have set out the philosophical, social and economic challenge of our times, and briefly examined two contrasting but inadequate responses. I have then made a proposal of an approach that seems more fitting for such a time as this. The rest of this book will outline and explore that proposal in more detail.

Notes

1 See *The Edinburgh Review*, 81, at https://books.google.ch/
books?id=cWFKAQAAMAAJ&pg=PA555&lpg=PA555&d-
q=The+Church+as+it+now+stands+no+human+power+-
can+save.&source=bl&ots=gzcyA_oihm&sig=n1v5VINDkIamO-
SZx-TixM4s8ves&hl=en&sa=X&ved=2ahUKEwjaqfmC8cnfAhU-
JtosKHX2WAYAQ6AEwAnoECAcQAQ#v=onepage&q=The%20
Church%20as%20it%20now%20stands%20no%20human%20
power%20can%20save.&f=false.

2 G. K. Chesterton, *What's Wrong with the World,* first published
in 1910.

3 J. Milbank and A. Pabst, *The Politics of Virtue: Postliberalism and
the Human Future* (London: Rowman & Littlefield, 2016).

4 Milbank and Pabst, p. 45.

5 Milbank and Pabst, p. 81.

6 Milbank and Pabst, p. 13.

7 Milbank and Pabst, p. 58.

8 Milbank and Pabst, p. 247.

9 Milbank and Pabst, pp. 274–5.

10 Milbank and Pabst, p. 21.

11 Milbank and Pabst, p. 69.

12 Milbank and Pabst, p. 85.

13 Milbank and Pabst, p. 78.

14 Milbank and Pabst, pp. 205–6.

15 Milbank and Pabst, p. 193.

16 M. Ignatieff, *The Ordinary Virtues: Moral Order in a Divided
World* (Cambridge, MA: Harvard University Press, 2017).

17 Ignatieff, p. 203.

18 Ignatieff, p. 208.

19 Ignatieff, p. 202.

20 Ignatieff, p. 9.

21 Ignatieff, p. 8.

22 Ignatieff, p. 202.

23 Ignatieff, p. 203.

24 Ignatieff, p. 52.

25 Ignatieff, pp. 28–9.

26 C. Kelly and B. Sheppard, 'Creating Common Purpose', *Global
Solutions Journal*, 1 (1), 2018: 80–7.

27 D. Snower (2017), 'The Dangerous Decoupling', retrieved from
www.g20-insights.org/wp-content/uploads/2017/05/The-Dangerous-
Decoupling.pdf, p. 1.

28 C. Kelly and B. Sheppard (2017), 'Common Purpose: Realigning
Business, Economies and Society', retrieved from www.strategy-business

.com/feature/Common-Purpose-Realigning-Business-Economies-and-Society?gko=e57f6.

29 Snower, 'The Dangerous Decoupling', p. 1.

30 Snower, p. 2.

31 D. Snower, 'Recoupling', in *Global Solutions Journal*, I (1), 2018: pp. 11–12.

32 Snower, 'The Dangerous Decoupling', p. 7.

33 Snower, p. 7.

34 C. Taylor, *A Secular Age* (Cambridge, MA: The Belknap Press of Harvard University Press, 2007), pp. 1–3.

35 Taylor, pp. 6–7.

Investing in the Kingdom: The Divine Economy

I'm going to take my argument in four stages. I'm going to start by suggesting that the New Testament call to discipleship is an all-embracing thing, that following Jesus requires our heart and mind and soul and strength. I'm then going to look at how the church has found it hard to live that call in practice, and has adapted its ways to what we might call a partial approach. Then I'm going to suggest that any solution to the churches' present woes about money that are based on a partial approach are unlikely to succeed, given that they are seeking to restore what I take to be a flawed model. Finally, I shall suggest what might be a renewed all-embracing model that might give hope and reignite the imagination of our conversation about money.

Two influential models

For our discussion of money, there's only one place to start. And that's with Jesus' call to discipleship: 'Follow me.' The Gospels play out the implications of Jesus' apparently simple invitation. For Jesus it means the formation of a community of committed disciples, sharing with them his trials and challenges as well as his wisdom and instruction; it means fellowship with those on whom the world has turned its back, both abiding among them and allowing his presence alongside an individual to change that person's life or circumstances for ever; and it means coming into conflict with those in authority – those who are holding the people of God to ransom and those who are keeping the coming kingdom of God in chains. This threefold ministry calls for threefold imitation: disciples are called to belong to an accountable community that stays close to Jesus, listens to his voice and seeks to know his ways; they are called to be with the poor, sharing the experience of exclusion, allowing their lives to be changed by encounter with those in whom Christ promised to show his face, and on occasion finding ways to offer tangible assistance as people change their own reality for the better; and they are called to come into lively encounter with those in authority, holding such people to account and looking for their conversion or for their rediscovery of God's kingdom and its expectations.

Jesus' call to leave material security behind is uncompromising and persistent. He has no time for a person who wants first to bury his father, or who wants to keep his talent safely buried in the ground, or who has just bought a piece of land and must go out and see it, or who has bought five yoke of oxen and is going to try them out, or who has just got married and is preoccupied. In this context, his celebrated encounter with the young man variously described as rich, or a ruler, stands out as a stark moment in a consistent trajectory. Jesus says to the man, 'Go, sell what you own, and give the money to the poor, and you will have treasure in heaven; then come, follow me' (Mark 10.21). As one commentator puts it:

> The two obligations – that this man should sell what he has and therefore become free for God, and that he should give it to the poor and therefore become free for his neighbour – both derive their meaning and force from this final demand, that he should come and follow Jesus.[1]

It's often pointed out that it was hard for the man to part with things to which he was very much attached. But we don't often ask, how was he to live once he'd done so?

This is a question that was focused in the ministry of St Francis of Assisi. Francis responded to Jesus' uncompromising call by making himself socially vulnerable and divesting himself of political and military power. What Francis was doing was taking Jesus' radical summons and turning it into a social vision that at the same time renewed the church. Francis' begging was about publicly calling forth gifts that would reveal Christ's church. At the same time, he was developing a form of social holiness based not on exchange and competition but on voluntary sacrifice and charity. His renunciation of property meant he could never be drawn into the most common form of social conflict: one that arises when one person defends their property rights against another's. His poverty was 'a form of economic unilateral disarmament'.[2]

St Francis goes, sells, gives to the poor, and then comes and follows Jesus. Simple as that. And within the conscience of many clergy, I would guess, if not within the conscience of most of the lay people they serve, is a nagging suspicion that perhaps they should be doing the same – for this is what the true imitation of Christ looks like. But it turned out not to be so simple for the Franciscans. Francis' model was poisoned by its own popularity. If godly poverty was the highest status, all worldly (and especially churchly) hierarchies were under threat; if the world was awash with voluntary beggars, not only were economic beggars displaced, but begging became a new marketplace of rhetoric and deceit. This was a realm not of God but of anarchy and scandalous abuse, as the fourteenth-century poem *Piers Plowman* exposes. The church's gifts, notably confession, had become a racket.

But the model of St Francis and Jesus' words to the rich young ruler are not the only words that have had a hold on the church's imagination when it comes to money. Equally influential are these words from Acts 2:

> They devoted themselves to the apostles' teaching and fellowship, to the breaking of bread and the prayers.
>
> Awe came upon everyone, because many wonders and signs were being done by the apostles. All who believed were

together and had all things in common; they would sell their possessions and goods and distribute the proceeds to all, as any had need. Day by day, as they spent much time together in the temple, they broke bread at home and ate their food with glad and generous hearts, praising God and having the goodwill of all the people. And day by day the Lord added to their number those who were being saved. (Acts 2.42–47)

'All who believed were together and had all things in common; they would sell their possessions and goods and distribute the proceeds to all, as any had need.' Not your average church council meeting. It's worth breaking this ideal picture down into its constituent elements. There is first the discovery of and formation in faith (the apostles' teaching). Then there is time spent with one another, building one another up and deepening support and encouragement (fellowship). Third, there is sacramental worship (the breaking of bread), and, fourth, there are other dimensions of worship (the prayers). Fifth, there are amazing acts of God, which bring awe on everyone. Sixth, there is the sharing of goods with one another, and, seventh, there is the selling of goods and distribution to those in need. And that's about it. The tangible results are goodwill among the people and a growth in the size of the community. In the background is the story of the feeding of the 5,000, and the constant sense that the church is more than the sum of its parts – that, with Jesus, scarcity becomes abundance.

This image has a powerful hold on the imagination of many Christians. There's a perpetual sense that, if we were doing it properly, we'd be sharing washing machines and having childcare cooperatives and sitting down for constant community meals. But it's important to note that this is a different picture from Jesus' words to the rich young man. The rich young man model is about living vulnerably before God and simply following Jesus. The Acts 2 model is about making a collective commitment and finding the activity of the Holy Spirit in the worship and practices of a community. Both models are compelling, but they're not the same. The two dominant kinds of medieval monasticism – the mendicant friars and the wealthy monasteries – represented these two poles of engaging with the ideal of somehow getting money right. The mendicant friars imitated the rich young man, and the Benedictine monasteries imitated the Acts 2 ideal community. But both models turned out to be flawed when translated into a vision for a whole society. The friars evoked anarchy, while the monasteries generated corruption, wealth and hypocrisy. Nonetheless, many clergy and others feel, deep down, they ought to have gone, sold up, given to the poor, and come and followed Jesus, living a simple life of prayer and service and relying on alms. Meanwhile, many Christian communities aspire to a noble ideal of shared possessions or at least in part a common purse.

The two models in the Reformation

So that's my first point. The gospel call is for wholehearted commitment, in a way that transcends conventional notions of family and ignores preoccupations about making a living. It offers two compelling models, itinerant mendicancy and intense community, that are not wholly compatible with one another, but were in different ways lived out in the Middle Ages and still have a hold on the church's imagination about money today.

My second point is that for the most part the church has found these two models too challenging to be implemented and too disruptive to be sustainable, not least because they dismantle familial and economic expectations that the church over the centuries has felt it couldn't live without. Two other models have emerged that broadly encompass the church's consensus about money. The first and earlier is what we might call the benefactor model. The logic of the benefactor model goes like this. I am not willing or able to make the kind of commitment of the monk or the mendicant. But I want the church to flourish, I want to be close to God, and I want myself and my loved ones to go to heaven. So I will subcontract the achievement of these goals to those who have made such all-encompassing commitments, and I will finance their flourishing. The epitome of the benefactor model is the medieval practice of saying Masses for the dead. Churches, and especially monasteries, grew, flourished and came to rely on income from precisely this source. But more generally the benefactor model is tied in to a class structure of squirearchy, an ethos of noblesse oblige and a dualist material–spiritual divide where the church in general and the clergy more specifically exist in large part to cleanse the earthy, fleshly world of its more unrefined qualities and make it fit to stand before God.[3]

Consider a conventional village church fundraising campaign. The regular congregation may be small and their resources not infinite. They have two sources of appeal: to the wider village and to the occupier of the sprawling Old Rectory or ancient restored Manor House. Both of these appeals rest on a benefactor model. They both assume a vicarious structure, in which non-churchgoers value the presence of the church building and regular worship in the community and wish to see it continue even if they anticipate playing little or no part in it. This isn't a chantry system, involving the payment of considerable sums for the saying of Masses for the dead, but it's on a continuum with that previous system. The message is still that we are doing something not just for ourselves but also for you. The role of the parish priest, particularly in village communities, still rests on benefactor assumptions. For example, the expectation of parish visiting is culturally and historically tied to the understanding that the priest had access to benevolent funds that could turn pastoral concern for the afflicted into material assistance for their well-being. Benefaction rests on a social system dominated by class, patronage and relationships of unspoken obligation.

The other model that has shaped the imagination of the church precisely because it doesn't demand wholehearted commitment is what we may call the stewardship model. You can't understand the stewardship model unless you grasp the degree to which the Reformation laicized the church. Prior to the Reformation, the normative ethical agent was a monk or a priest. After the Reformation, the normative ethical agent became a layperson who owned disposable wealth and most likely was engaged in profitable business. Christianity was democratized – or at least made a bourgeois phenomenon. The conventional vocation was to use God's beneficence to care effectively for human needs. If one were to experience growth or increase one should consider such blessings characteristic of that effectiveness. The crucial thing to notice is that Jesus' words to the rich young man drop out of the scene altogether. Poverty, voluntary or communal, is ruled out. 'Since persons do not own goods but are given charge of them for efficient use, renunciation is a refusal to take up the moral responsibility God has given people.'[4]

It's interesting to note that stewardship is a peculiarly English word: Spanish, for example, has no single term for the concept, and German sometimes simply italicizes the English word 'steward'.[5] In Tyndale's 1534 translation of the New Testament, the term 'steward' is used only once. But the concept had taken hold by the eighteenth century, largely because of the influence of John Wesley. Wesley's famous slogan was 'Gain all you can; save all you can; give all you can'[6]. Kelly Johnson notes:

> As a guideline for determining what to use on oneself, Wesley teaches people to consider themselves simply the first in a number of poor they must care for. Hence, a Christian should care for himself or herself as for the poor, by tending to necessities and nothing beyond . . . The kind of renunciation that would make a person a beggar is considered reprehensible, for one's first duty is to (frugal) self-preservation. As Wesley noted, admitting himself to be rich, it is not possessing wealth, but possessing more than is employed according to God's will that is the problem.[7]

As he vividly put it, 'If I leave behind me ten pounds (above my debts and the little arrears of my fellowship) you and all mankind bear witness against me that "I lived and died a thief and a robber."[8]

Wesley's nineteenth-century successors, particularly in the United States, took this healthy legacy in two significant directions. The narrative of the man who grew wealthier after he made a commitment to give generously attained mythic dimensions; and Wesley's insistence that the wealth must be gained justly fades from the scene.[9] But notice this rules out voluntary or communal poverty altogether. If we have no money, we can't care for the poor, as a Methodist named Margaret Thatcher once famously pointed out.

So this is my second point. The two compelling scriptural models were replaced by two alternative models that suited the sociology of the church in different times. Just as Francis had adopted the individual character of the Mark 10 model, so the benefactor took on the same mantle in a new, less sacrificial age. And just as the Benedictines had taken on the Acts 2 model in the Middle Ages, so after the Reformation the steward became the representative of collective action in pursuit of a common goal. These two models didn't make the demands of the two scriptural models; they recognized that people sought to live conventional lives, with families, careers, regular sources of income and perhaps even some habits of life that sat outside the church's official ethic. But these two models have given us the church we have today.

The two models today

My third point is that it may be that these two models have run their course. If one were to try to diagnose the money question as it pervades the sleepless nights of those responsible for church finance on a local, regional or national level, one might put it like this: the established church was largely founded, and for many centuries run, on the benefactor model. Some decades ago the sums ceased to add up. It's important to note that this isn't primarily about real or perceived falls in congregation size, because under the benefactor model congregation size isn't especially important in how money works in the church. It's about sociological changes, such as how long retired clergy live, what constitutes reasonable provision for people in their retirement, whether the noblesse feel as obliged as they used to, given that the ancient aristocracy are not so fixed in their estates as they once were, and the shift of the majority of the population to cities, where relationships of unspoken obligation are different from the abiding practice of the country.

In the last two or three generations, a church whose money rested fundamentally on the system and legacy of squirearchy has morphed into a church that rests on congregationalism. By congregationalism I mean the assumption that the basic unit of Christianity is the local church, that each local church should seek to be self-sufficient as regards the provision of its stipendiary ministry, building upkeep and additional administrative and liturgical costs, and that those costs should be met almost entirely through the voluntary stewardship of members of its congregation. I want to point out that this kind of congregationalism is a new development for the established church, that, while it has many good features, it also has some negative side-effects, and that the increasingly evident failure of this model to deliver what the church currently needs should not be a cause of wistful lament or hand-wringing despair but a call to a renewal of the church through the catalyst of money.

Let's start with the good features. Congregationalism is a long way from the Acts 2 model of holding all things in common. But it does set up a healthy dynamism by which people practise their faith that God has given them everything they need to worship and follow in the way of Jesus Christ. At its best, congregationalism affirms that money is always God's, not ours, that the more one gives, the more one cares, and that giving makes the relationships of community essential. Giving the first, significant, percentage of one's income certainly pays for the administration of the Christian community, underwriting its expenses, supporting its mission and alleviating hardship; and such giving frequently demonstrates sacrificial love, answering and echoing the sacrificial love of God. But deeper than that, and at its very best, congregational stewardship discloses that money is always a gift, always an instrument, to serve a greater end – and never a goal, never an end in itself. Money becomes a means of establishing and maintaining relationships, rather than a method of bypassing relationships, or an insurance in case relationships go wrong. Its primary purpose is to engraft disciples in community, by transforming their politics from the politics of scarcity (paying the bills) to a politics of abundance. In deliberating over how to invest the surplus gifts of God, the community learns to identify the places and ways God works in the world, and how best to follow where God has led. The translation of common faith and common vision into a common purse concentrates the minds and hearts of disciples such that every gift they make is evaluated for faithfulness and accompanied by prayer.

Beyond building community and deepening faith, the other good feature of congregational stewardship is its simplicity and transparency. If the complex commands and expectations of discipleship are confusing and bewildering, it's a great relief to be told, 'Tithe your pre-tax earnings' – or even your post-tax earnings – 'and regard that as a minimum standard for your giving in general.' And it's pretty obvious whether people are doing so or not. There's a lot to be said for prayerful consideration of how much to give; but there's even more to be said for a simple commitment to give 10 per cent and not go into the details. Just take the issue off your desk. We can't live life in a whirlwind of choice: some of the biggest things in life are those we just decide to do and stick to.

If those are the positive features of congregational stewardship, the negative features come down to three, and they're all characteristics of money matters in general. First is the tendency to shrink the mission of the church to the priorities of those with the largest wallets. One reason the mainline denominations in the USA are in perpetual tension is that most of their clergy take a progressive view of issues surrounding sexuality, while many members with the largest wallets take a more conservative view. Whatever one's commitments around sexuality questions in the church today, it can't be right that one simply gets the doctrine one pays for. But in a congregational model it's almost inevitable that those who give the most assume they get to shout the loudest. Second is that the more self-sufficient a congregation becomes the more irrelevant the diocese or oversight body seems to be. Almost inevitably the parish share comes to feel like a tax, and a financially healthy congregation comes to affiliate more closely with those of a like mind than with others of a similar postcode and under the same bishop. What this means is that by promoting congregational stewardship in the last three generations the diocese or oversight body has been almost unavoidably advancing its own perceived irrelevance.

Third is the assumption, indeed the conviction, that stewardship is fundamentally about money. In John Wesley's view, money is 'that precious talent which contains all the rest'. Through the mechanism of money, he believed, people might exercise all six works of mercy set out in Matthew 25.[10] But, as I've already suggested, money is never more than a device for creating relationships, and once one has those relationships, the money is secondary. God's abundance is located in the relationships, not in the money. I consider myself blessed to have had seven years' experience of living in a culture where the church has all the things the church in the UK thinks it needs – numbers, money and social influence. But it turns out that the kingdom of God is no closer. What I discovered from seven years living in the American South is that numbers, money and influence are as often an obstacle to discovering the grace and kingdom of God as they are an entry point.

The established church is in a financial plight for one simple reason. It once worked with a benefactor model that affirmed hierarchies, enshrined mixed motives, was hopelessly tied to an outdated class and patronage system, and yet directed the church's attention to the whole parish, the whole nation and the wider goods of the kingdom. But it has shifted somewhat abruptly to a different model. This new model, the stewardship model, can galvanize a congregation, but tends to narrow the notion of mission, impoverish the texture of a diocese and overvalue the power of money compared to relationship. And the new model doesn't pay the bills. But I don't believe this should be a cause for unbounded lament because I'm not sure it was a truly scriptural model in the first place.

How it should work

There's nothing fundamentally wrong with a conventional approach to congregational giving that appeals to three dimensions – God, church and kingdom. Such an approach starts by dismantling the question, 'Why should I spend my money on the church?' Such a question is based on a misunderstanding. The first mistake is to speak of 'my' money. Property rights are a convention of civilized society – but they're fundamentally based on a falsehood. Things don't belong to us. They belong to God. Like everything else, money is something we look after for a while, but can't ultimately keep. The choice is not whether to hang on to it or give it away, it's who to give it to.

That's why the word 'spend' is also wrong. 'Spend' is a verb that offers a sense of power, a sense of executive control that can make things happen or acquire possessions by dispensing money. But that's not what happens. What people actually do is to invest money. Every act that we call spending is in fact taking a risk, that this bar of chocolate will make us happy, that this newspaper will keep us informed and entertained, that this car will be more worth than it is trouble, that this house will be a comfort and not a millstone. If we use the word 'spend', we hide the reality of that risk. If we replace 'spend' with 'invest' then we recognize we can't control the outcomes of our risky ventures, and we broaden our imaginations to consider what really lasts for ever. And that leads us to God, because 'God' is more or less synonymous with 'for ever'. Christians believe in a personal God, but the most basic understanding of God would be 'that which lasts for ever'. If we're in the investment business, which we all are, why wouldn't we invest in that which lasts for ever? It makes all other investment look absurdly short-term.

If we return to the question, 'Why should I spend my money on the church?', another word that's wrong is 'should'. Giving isn't a guilt trip. It's a recognition that no one can buy the things that really matter – love, joy, peace and, finally, salvation. If they were for sale, no one would be able to afford them, not even the 1 per cent of the world that are richer than the rest put together. Love, joy and peace are glorious gifts, and they've been given not to those who deserve them but to people like us who squander them all the time. God has given us everything we need. We can spend our money either out of gratitude or in constructing an impregnable empire that doesn't need God. That's not about 'should' – about duty, about obligation. That's about overflow, about joy, about celebrating amazing grace. The law of exchange, where one person has goods and services and another person buys them, only works for transitory things. When we're dealing with 'for ever' we need to revert to another system. And the name of that system is 'gift'. The more you transfer resources from the market economy into the gift economy, the more you're starting to enter eternal life. It's not about duty, it's about joy.

It's as well to acknowledge that this goes against many instincts we're born with, like self-preservation, and many habits we're trained in, like putting oneself first. Here lies the significance of John Wesley's advice, 'Consider yourself the first among the poor you are called to serve.' It recognizes that we have deep, pressing and real needs, and only when those needs are met can we relax and live for others. But it assumes that these needs can be met, and life isn't about amassing more and more wealth, comfort and security to keep the ravages of the world at bay. The economy of gift believes that generosity is the best investment. Hoarding goods and living in constant anxiety is, in the end, idolatry because it's investing too much worth in something less than God. It's not so much wrong, as foolish and sad.

Then there is the word 'church'. The word 'church' is wrong if it's taken to mean something that's separate from ourselves and separate from God. Those who believe in the economy of gift – investing in for ever – want to be part of the body of Christ, the embodiment of eternal grace. So all their money should lie with the church, minus the part they hold back as they consider themselves first among the poor they're called to serve. But that's incomprehensible if it isn't simply a way of investing in God. That doesn't mean not paying taxes, because taxes provide the ordered government that makes freedom possible and the basic services that make life liveable. It doesn't mean not giving to charities, because charities provide the concrete acts of mercy for which a majority in a democracy would not vote. It doesn't mean living a life of begging and destitution, because Jesus instructs us to love not only God and our neighbour but also ourselves, and loving ourselves is part of the way we show our gratitude to God. But it does mean that for Christians their whole lives are oriented to the economy of gift and investing in for ever, and the word for the place where gift and for ever meet is church. There's nothing more inspiring than being among a bunch of people who have committed to living in the economy of grace and invested in church and are resting on the providence of God. God isn't a distant and arbitrary landlord who is twice a year summoned to fix the plumbing. God is the one who's invested everything in the church and who invites the church to invest everything in return. If faith isn't alive, it's usually because little has been invested in it.

Church is not just a tangible way to invest in God. It's a tangible way people invest in each other. It's sometimes a cause of lament that spouses and partners argue so much about money – but it's inevitable, because money is the most tangible way people identify and demonstrate what they value in life. Those with whom we share a bank account is a bigger social statement than those with whom we share a bed. Sharing a bank account means you have to explain and fight and persuade and ask and beg and share and forgive, which are all the things that make a relationship. They're also all the things that make a church.

Church is supposed to be a herald and advance foretaste of kingdom. Whether it employs one person or several, it needs to practise what it preaches. Few congregations in the UK are rich. Most congregation members have followed a path in life that brought no great financial reward, or have faced obstacles in life that depleted what resources they might otherwise have accrued. But kingdom means things like greater income equality, environmental sustainability, fair trade. To bring such things about in our nation requires huge political will, which we can hope and pray and strive to foster. But to practise such things in a church requires additional investment. There's only one way to do that – and that's for congregational giving to fill the gap in the balance sheet created by the church's trying to turn its convictions into action. A congregation can't call for government, business and civil society to live its values unless it's prepared to face the cost of living them itself.

A new model

There's only really one thing wrong with this conventional appeal. It doesn't work. At least, it doesn't work in the large majority of congregations in the UK today. It's time for a new approach.

Let's put together what we've seen in the argument so far. The two scriptural models are demanding because they dismantle conventional familial and economic expectations that the church over the centuries felt it couldn't live without. They have always been practised by a minority, and still are today. In place of them the church pursued two other models, that of benefactor and steward, which fitted more comfortably with the familial and economic realities the church was resolved to accept. These are the models that are coming to grief today. We talk as if they were the only models. But they are both profoundly flawed, and neither does full justice to the way the Bible talks about money as the stimulus to the renewal of relationships, rather than a mechanism for navigating the shortcomings of relationships. If we return to the Gospels, for example in the parable of the steward in Luke 16, we can see

Jesus inaugurating an inspiring transformation in relationships that's stimulated by, but not limited to, a transformation in the use of money.

Walter Brueggemann offers six theses for a scriptural understanding of money and possessions. Money and possessions, he says, (1) are gifts from God; (2) are received as reward for obedience; (3) belong to God and are held in trust by human beings in community; (4) are sources of social injustice; (5) are to be shared in a neighbourly way; (6) are seductions that lead to idolatry.[11] Thus an ethic of money begins with gratitude. Pharaoh forgot this, and thought, 'My Nile is my own; I made it for myself' (Ezek. 29.3) – whereas in truth the Nile had made him. Likewise, living in the rhythm of God and delight in God's companionship generally yields fruit; but this is a relationship of trust. It contrasts with 'a market ideology in which there are no free lunches and no glad gratitude but only payouts for performance and production'.[12] In 2 Samuel 3.12, the general Abner asks David, 'To whom does the land belong?' Like Abner, in seizing Naboth's vineyard Ahab later assumes the land belongs to the king. But in truth the land always belongs to God; and forgetting this is the root cause of much social injustice in the Old Testament. Jesus' indication that we are to find him in the hungry, thirsty, naked, stranger, sick and prisoner are in the same tradition of Isaiah's words that a true fast is to share bread with the hungry, bring the homeless poor into one's house, and cover the naked (Isa. 58.7). Deuteronomy warns that if the people have too much silver and gold, they will turn them into an idol, just as takes place in the construction of the golden calf, and just as brings down Belshazzar at his feast in Daniel 5. The point for our discussion is that money should be a means to an end, but all too often becomes an end; thus the way money is raised, more than the amount raised, becomes a vital sign of the health of a community.

What does this mean for us as a church? Well, there's no reason to give up on benefaction and stewardship straight away. They both have their place and they may function differently in rural and urban areas, in gathered and neighbourhood contexts. The conventional appeal that I offered earlier is still right in almost every respect; it abides by the scriptural theses Brueggemann lays out. But there is also this principle: God gives us the abundance of the kingdom to renew the poverty of the church. In other words, if the church is a cul-de-sac or a quagmire, it's time to invest in the kingdom.

The experience of one congregation may be instructive. At St Martin-in-the-Fields in London, the benefactor model was still in place longer than most urban churches. Built by George I in a blend of architectural styles to affirm the union of England and Scotland in 1707, and especially of Britain and Hanover in 1714, the vicars of St Martin's had generally been well connected. A timely call to a grandee, even a royal, in times of hardship would tide things over till the next shortfall. By the 1980s the sums didn't add up. The costs of the building and the extensive outreach ministry far exceeded the (albeit significantly under-tapped) potential of congregational stewardship. The answer was to create a commercial enterprise. The then vicar, Geoffrey Brown, had long been interested in the workplace, not just as a source of income; he and his team were flexible in trying out ways the church buildings might be made amenable to generating significant profits.

The results a generation later have been remarkable. St Martin's has been able to maintain and expand its ability to extend its mission well beyond the imaginations of its wealthiest and most generous members and donors. But there's more to it than that. Originally the food services, retail, events and commercial concerts were seen in largely instrumental terms, to underwrite the lofty spiritual mission and ministry of the church. But what's happened is that the business has ended up teaching the congregation a lot about the kingdom. The commercial enterprise with its 120 staff from 25 countries is a microcosm of a multicultural society. Meanwhile, St Martin's now sees itself as a community of hope, reimagining church and society through culture, charity, commerce and congregational life. It's a vision of a civil economy, of what work and play, friendship and worship, social concern and evangelism, diversity and identity might look like.

St Martin's has the advantage of being in Trafalgar Square and having a huge quantity of tourist traffic. This also brings disadvantages: a huge cost of building maintenance and security, a large insurance bill, and occasions when the agenda of a major outdoor public gathering space dictates what's possible indoors. But flourishing life is not all about existing potential. Look at Switzerland: no natural resources, so it tries banking and watches. But the point I want to stress is that St Martin's success has come out of adversity, out of near bankruptcy. The financial imperative proved to be a good thing: it renewed the church. And the business is now an integral part of the church's life. If you have senior staff members who are Jewish or Muslim, you don't say they're staff subcontracted to deliver services: they're wearing a St Martin-in-the-Fields polo shirt like everyone else, and St Martin's has to adapt its notion of church to accommodate the kingdom that God is giving it. That kingdom is about living God's future now: modelling in social relations the activities and company the church anticipates in heaven.

The sociological point is this. In 1948 a revolution took place in this country in which the state became the church. The state took over a lot of the things the church used to do. The church had to decide what it was going to be. It chose to reinvent itself as offering something called spirituality. And what happened was that it ceased to require the services of those whose spirituality was more practically oriented. And the people most churches attract are for the most part those who are happy to receive spirituality; but churches no longer see those who find perfect freedom in doing practical things. St Martin's still sees such people, because it still has voluntary and paid jobs for them to do. Today the state is having second thoughts. It isn't at all sure it wants to be the church any more. It's a really exciting time to be the church. But in order to enjoy its possibilities the church has to believe it's about more than spirituality, and it has to let its financial needs and the material poverty of many it encounters become entry points to new adventures, new relationships, new discoveries in God's kingdom. For example, just imagine if a rural parish didn't go cap in hand to the neo-gentry in the Old Vicarage once in every four years looking for £10,000 to help with a new church roof but instead asked for a loan of a project manager to create a business plan to make a sustainable income for the congregation. It might give the resident of the Old Vicarage a worthy place to locate a loyal employee close to retirement; but more broadly, it could galvanize the whole village to get behind a common project. Either way, it would be likely to elicit a much more engaged response from the Old Vicarage.

The Old Testament was written because God's people in exile found it not a time of despair but one of renewal, not a time simply of losing the land but more wonderfully of gaining a new and deeper relationship with God. The New Testament was written because the early Christians found that the execution of their Lord and Saviour was not the end of the story but the beginning, that his agony was the foretaste of glory, that his killers meant it for evil but God meant it for good. The logic is clear: let's take this time of financial heart-searching in our church and see it as a gift from the Holy Spirit, a gift for the clarifying of the gospel, the renewing of the church and the rediscovery of the kingdom. Make money your friend in the business of making friends, remember that generosity is the best investment, let God show you the kingdom – and let that kingdom renew the church.

Notes

1 Karl Barth, *Church Dogmatics* II/2 (Edinburgh: T&T Clark, 2009), p. 622, quoted in Kevin Hargaden, *Theological Ethics in a Neoliberal Age Confronting the Christian Problem with Wealth* (Eugene, OR: Cascade, 2018), p. 52.

2 Kelly Johnson, *The Fear of Beggars: Stewardship and Poverty in Christian Ethics* (Grand Rapids: Eerdmans, 2007), p. 24.

3 It's worth noting that Jesus himself had benefactors (Luke 8.3).

4 Johnson, *The Fear of Beggars*, p. 84.

5 Johnson, p. 73.

6 Sermon 87; II.8, paraphrased.

7 Johnson, *The Fear of Beggars*, p. 86.

8 John Wesley, *An Earnest Appeal to Men of Reason and Religion* (1743), 96, in *Works* 11:87–88.

9 Johnson, *The Fear of Beggars*, p. 92.

10 Johnson, p. 85.

11 Walter Brueggemann, *Money and Possessions* (Louisville: Westminster John Knox Press, 2016), pp. 1–11.

12 Brueggemann, pp. 3–4.

3

Minding God's Business:
Becoming a Parable

I set out to address three questions in this chapter. First, is there something inherently problematic in church getting too tangled up in business? Surely there must be a good reason why it isn't very common. Perhaps that reason lies in some deep-seated incompatibility, identified in the Bible but easily overlooked, or maybe the issue is whether the church should set its face against the all-pervading tide of neoliberalism. Second, if there is such a thing as the business of the kingdom, what kind of business might that involve, and what are its purposes? Third, what is the potential for a kingdom business movement within the vision of church renewal set out thus far in my first two chapters?

Do we have a problem?

In the UK, the biggest conceptual issue to overcome in understanding how church and business can coincide is a struggle to disentangle three things that are easily confused.

First, the popular image of church, among insiders and outsiders, is a cheerful one of a sleepy vicar or minister, a part-time secretary and a working party every few months to dig out the churchyard and clear the gutters. This dovetails with the widespread notion of Christianity as otherworldly, absent-minded, harmless, hapless and homespun, as found in *The Vicar of Dibley* and *Dad's Army*. By contrast, a second is an image of business as a tight ship, a culture of money and success, and the power, influence and often ruthlessness that come with them. For a lot of people such things are always suspicious and usually bad, and a church is an easier place to relate to when it's hand-to-mouth, happy-go-lucky and less transparent about how it pays its bills. There's a lingering memory that Jesus drove money-changers out of the temple, and for some this invalidates commercial activity altogether; but most people realize he was condemning the exploitation of the poor and the instrumentalization of religion for profiteering, rather than discrediting business itself: after all, his family were carpenters. And the third element is the fear that if church gets too tangled up with business, the culture of business may obscure or even displace what has historically been the heart of what is meant by church – a living, worshipping, witnessing Christian community.

It's in this last element, the sense that business is all very well but is somehow not really church, that the key anxiety resides. Consider the word 'business'. It's obviously derived from busy-ness, the state of being frenetic, occupied, all-of-a-busy. Here we have to acknowledge a philosophical and class-based distinction that goes back to classical times. In Latin the word *otium* means leisure. The word for business is *negotium*, which means not-leisure. For the ancients, the contemplative life was the highest aspiration: when Socrates said, 'The unexamined life is not worth living', he placed in the imagination of the West the idea that busy-ness was not only undesirable but unworthy. This can play into a dualism that's found in a lot of Christianity – a dualism that drives a wedge between the worldly body and the otherworldly soul, and assumes spirituality is about escaping from the flesh and seeking the spirit.

The incarnation and bodily resurrection of Jesus discredit this kind of dualism because they show that God in Christ is utterly invested in our physical being and that our life with God for ever will be a physical, tangible one. The account of the capable wife in Proverbs 31 dismantles any sentimentality about a precious, trophy, leisured existence, and praises the woman who rolls up her sleeves and plants and reaps and wheels and deals and acquires wisdom, strength and dignity. The parable of the talents in Matthew 25 criticizes the slave who thought that all the master wanted was his intangible love, and praises the slaves who got into the marketplace and made that love real and took risks and found rewards. Likewise, George Herbert's hymn 'Teach me, my God and king' is a prayer to find joy in daily tasks and turn business into ministry by placing it in the hands of God.

A healthy society is not one that relegates work and business to the secondary out-house of trade while exalting worship and prayer at the top table of piety. Instead, a healthy life seeks a rhythm of work, home life, nurture, rest, witness, service and play, looking to worship, formation, personal devotion and fellowship to inform and transform at every stage. Business requires imagination, commitment, competitiveness, alertness, care, skill, teamwork, wisdom, timing, energy, partnership, leadership, loyalty and drive. These are all good, created, blessed and worthy things – goods in themselves, and not just a means to the end of profit and making a living. If one had a million pounds, one could give it away to a charity; but it might be better to set up or develop a business that gave livelihood, companionship and flourishing life to a whole network of people, while generating revenue for government and offering dignity to a community.

Are we part of a larger problem?

It may be said that the church needs to wake up to the social and economic climate in which it lives, and regard business with suspicion for more sophisticated reasons.

While the critique of capitalism goes back at least as far as Karl Marx, a somewhat different analysis has arisen in relation to the prevailing neoliberalism of the period since about 1980. Neoliberalism in broad terms is a theory that deeply respects private property rights, free markets and free trade, while conceiving of almost all human activity in terms of competition and efficiency. Thus neoliberalism has emerged as a totalizing system that 'aspires to a level of influence where nothing is *entirely* outside its domain'.[1] It begins to be almost impossible to imagine any coherent alternative. As Kevin Hargaden puts it, the totalizing effect of neoliberalism is observable

> in how it extends the logic of the market to parts of life that had previously operated on a different logic, in how it replaces the contention of political deliberation with the calculation of technical expertise, and, most critically, in how it colonizes how we think about the world, training us to be competitors concerned with self-interest and to aspire to self-destructive levels of comfort. It dominates our imagination.[2]

Hargaden reminds us of Martin Luther's account of the First Commandment in his *Larger Catechism*, where Luther writes:

> What is God? Answer: A God means that from which we are to expect all good and to which we are to take refuge in all distress, so that to have a God is nothing else than to trust and believe Him from the heart.[3]

Luther adds: 'the confidence and faith of the heart alone make both God and an idol.' By this measure, money has become the supreme value by which all other goods are measured, and capitalism is indeed, as Luther puts it, 'that from which we are to expect all good and to which we are to take refuge in all distress' – in other words, an unambiguous focus of idolatry.

The question thus arises, is a congregation succumbing to such idolatry if it presumes to enter the marketplace, or is it culpably naive if it believes it can participate in this realm without losing its identity and becoming a prisoner or an unconscious accomplice of it?

I have two contrasting answers to this question. The first is, almost the whole of western society is exposed to the potentially pernicious as well as the undoubtedly beneficial effects of capitalism. The idea that participating actively in the market makes a community vulnerable in a way it would otherwise be immune is the true naivety. It means subscribing to what is sometimes called the myth of clean money. As explained in Chapter 2, a congregation that doesn't generate its own income is simply subject to the contributions of those who have made their money in the very same market economy and almost inevitably share some or most of its values. There's no third option. That's not to say the congregation shouldn't be alert to seduction: market thinking must always be one means among many, and never be allowed to become an end. A church must continue to ensure all its language about people and purpose resists commodification and instrumentalization. The second answer is, surely the context of the dominance of neoliberal thinking requires more than ever examples of how a community may engage in business without making the market an idol. The alternative is a counsel of despair that recognizes our ultimate powerlessness in the face of the all-pervading market, thereby treating the market as a god just as much as if it were actively worshipped, and dolefully assuming all anyone could do would be to make ultimately futile gestures in the face of inevitable defeat.

Thus a brief acknowledgement of the context of neoliberal thinking only strengthens the urgency of offering positive, humble, constructive examples of business pursued with an end beyond competition and efficiency.

What kind of business?

I am going to assume that my arguments thus far have left the reader with an appetite to explore what a closer connection of church and business might involve. There are broadly three kinds of businesses available to congregations that wish to pursue commercial engagement in the spirit envisaged in this chapter:

1 *Instrumental.* Undertake a legitimate trading activity that has no direct social impact, make a profit, and then transfer that profit to other activities that do have direct social impact, whether simply the sustainability of the congregation and its building, or such mission projects as it pursues.

2 *Exemplary.* Undertake a trading activity that has no direct social impact, but seek to do so in an exemplary way, paying good wages, having a minimal environmental footprint, using locally generated resources, promoting fair trade practices, and so on, while still transferring profit to the activities mentioned under (1) above.

3 *Social.* Undertake a trading activity whose profit return is evidently secondary to the indirect social impact sought.

In the *instrumental* approach, the aim is simply to generate funds – funds that in some congregations might be supplied by congregational stewardship, or conventional voluntary fundraising such as the parish fête or dinner and auction. A congregation might embark on such an enterprise if it had a building that had very high upkeep costs, for example a listed building or one in a poor state of repair, or if the congregation had ambitions to purchase a building or increase the size and/or broaden the use of their building. There is no social impact foreseen in the activity itself: any legitimate business proposition can suffice. Offering employment may be one among the ancillary social benefits, but such benefits are incidental to the central purpose of generating a profit; and that distinction is accentuated if the business is subcontracted to a third party and the staff members are not directly employed by the congregation or its commercial subsidiary. It is accentuated further if practices of staff members or operating methods of the enterprise differ in significant ways from the ethos of the congregation; it's not hard, for example, to see a clash of views about the sale of alcohol if that were to be a primary form of income generation, or the appearance of books by the 'new atheists' if a bookstore were to be a part of the business.

When a congregation embarks on such an enterprise it makes two assumptions. One is that the venture will indeed make a profit. The other is that the profit will indeed be used to achieve the ministry or mission objectives envisaged, rather than, for example, be drawn upon to underwrite or invest in the business. In broad terms this approach is similar to the way a regular business disburses a proportion of its profit through its corporate social responsibility budget, how a foundation invests its endowment in financial markets, or how charities develop trading subsidiaries – thus the National Trust runs a large number of gift shops.

Turning to the *exemplary* approach, many of the same principles apply. The difference is that the congregation sees the enterprise not just as a cash cow to fund its ministry and mission, but as part of and in some cases integral to its ministry and mission. For that reason it accepts a lower financial return, because it regards some of what would have been profit as expenditure on ministry and mission. For example, if it maintains a policy of paying an optional local minimum wage, or assigning more-than-statutory sick pay, or giving its staff other such benefits, it is setting the costs of being an exemplary employer against other ministry and mission projects that could have been funded with the same money. (This leaves aside the argument that paying better wages makes for happier staff and consequently increased profits; and also the PR value and thus potential financial benefit of being known as a good employer.) To make this step is to challenge the conventional understanding of 'church' in a way the first approach need not. For example, can it still be described as mission and ministry if many or most of the people employed by the business aren't Christians? To answer 'no' to this question minimizes the power of the Holy Spirit. The Christian story is full of examples of how the Holy Spirit inspires people to further the kingdom beyond the imagination of the church. It wouldn't cross many Christians' minds to suggest that Christian Aid isn't doing mission, even though most people who work for Christian Aid worldwide aren't Christians. Having an open recruitment policy invites into the community a wondrously diverse, extraordinarily committed and endlessly fascinating body of people whose humility, hard work and integrity may well put the rest of the community to shame. The mistake is to concentrate on what perhaps isn't there instead of seeing what abundantly is there. An opportunity could be missed to create a living example of creative and dynamic unity in diversity without uniformity or exclusion – exactly what the United Kingdom's multicultural society as a whole is striving for.

In the *social* approach, the company has the appearance of a business, but the primary goal is to model the kingdom, by prioritizing social means as well as social ends. Thus the business may make a priority of employing those who are rough sleepers, for example a bike repair workshop where those who are currently homeless can regain confidence and work once again within structures. Alternatively, a venture may seek to train prisoners for work after their period of incarceration, perhaps as a chef or table attendant in a restaurant. For a congregation, this is simply mission; it doesn't need and can seldom aspire to be income-generating to any significant degree: but its metrics are not those of a conventional profit-and-loss account. The most challenging thing for a congregation can be to be clear in its expectations: it's not helpful to set up a business directed at raising profits, to hire staff equipped to do that and to market the venture accordingly, only for congregation members to lament that the business does not look like it's taking the social approach – when that was never the intention. The problem is not the sordidness of all commercial enterprise: it's about a failure to give clear instructions and set realistic expectations.

A subset of the social approach we might call the *balanced* approach.[4] In the balanced approach, there's no separation between the financial profits and the social impact. The two are of a piece. In many cases the company has to find a balance between generating financial returns and creating social impact. Examples include fair trade businesses and microfinance institutions: in such cases, the need to show a significant profit inevitably lessens the social benefit, at least in the short to medium term. A relatively unusual variant of this model is found where the financial returns and the social impact match each other. Examples include wind farms and organic vegetable box schemes. These are in many ways ideal social enterprises, because they both make a profit and have a significant social benefit, and the more benefit they generate the more profit they make. One can imagine that

> a clothing firm that pioneers the use of organic cotton is making a trade-off between financial and social returns. The firm could use non-organic cotton which would be cheaper, but less environmentally friendly (non-organic cotton crops represent one of the heaviest uses of pesticides in the world). Suppose, however, that the market eventually changes so that consumers end up preferring to buy only organic cotton clothing (and are prepared to pay more for it). In such a scenario, an 'ethical' clothing firm continues to use organic cotton and should make money by doing so.[5]

In purely financial terms, much the same things could be said of a congregation; the larger it gets, and in particular the more congregational giving it generates, the more it can do by way of ministry and mission. This is a crude form of measurement, but it is nonetheless the spoken or unspoken aspiration of most congregations.

The best fit

Having surveyed three kinds of business, and given examples of how they each work, in society and in the church, it's time for a brief review of which kind might be suitable for a congregation to adopt. The answer largely lies in the reasons that brought the congregation into this conversation in the first place.

A congregation that is broadly happy with its vision for ministry and mission, but finds it simply can't pay for the activity it feels called to sustain, is likely to go for the instrumental approach. A number of decisions will characterize what kind of business (and thus what relation to ministry and mission) is in view. Will the business take place on the same site as the church building? If not, it is easier to distinguish between the business and the congregation; indeed, it might be hard to make any connection at all; which might be a deliberate policy. For example, the congregation may come to own one or more properties that are rented out at a profit, or a share portfolio that is traded for significant returns. These are ways of keeping income streams largely invisible. By contrast, a church in a marketplace may sell land or property and build or convert a space into a cafe for use by the public. If such a cafe is sublet, the instrumental imperative is highlighted, and the congregation's leadership will need to keep a very close relationship with those running the cafe in order to anticipate, avoid and downplay any tensions of ethos or operation. If the cafe is run by the congregation or its trading subsidiary, it will almost inevitably need to migrate to the exemplary approach, since the staff will quickly and widely be regarded as representatives of the congregation, whether they see themselves that way or not.

There are good reasons why a congregation may wish to maintain an instrumental approach. If its ministry and mission are exemplary in every respect other than its ability to pay for them, it may choose to keep the large majority of its focus on its areas of strength. If its congregational capacity is small, and it doesn't see itself being able to cope with the management, governance and leadership requirements of employing a significant number of people, it may be wise not to do so. If the business conducted is a specialist one, and not widely understood, it may be best to subcontract it and 'leave it to the experts'. However, in most cases, especially when the business and the congregation share premises, the instrumental approach will be a temporary status, perhaps for the first few years while the enterprise becomes established, and the congregation's aspiration will be to integrate the business more fully with the life of the whole organization, which is what the exemplary approach seeks to do.

The exemplary approach is subject to many challenges. If a business seeks to pay its staff the living wage, and is in a sector where that is rare, it is putting itself at a commercial disadvantage against its competitors. If a venture is to adapt itself to market conditions, be ahead of the curve in its products and marketing, bring out the best in its staff, and have a dynamic plan for five years hence, it will need excellent senior management and talented non-executive directors; this will almost certainly entail attracting people of suitable background and ability from the wider church and community who (in the case of the directors) expect no reward but the pride of being part of a worthy cause or (in the case of the executives) could doubtless earn a higher salary elsewhere. If the marketing is unattractive, the product not good enough, the commercial climate challenging, or the whole concept flawed, the profit may be small or non-existent; people will be heard to say, 'This is not a charity' – when, in some ways, it is; while painful choices may need to be faced about those things that make up the term 'exemplary', and which ones need to be sacrificed first. There's no doubt people will be quick to point out the hubris of calling oneself exemplary, ignoring the difference between a fact and an aspiration. Even if it goes well, it can (like any aspect of ministry or mission) become an idol, absorbing all of some people's energies, to the detriment of their well-being or the wide calling of the congregation.

Notwithstanding these hazards, the exemplary approach is the best fit for most congregational commercial ventures. Like it or not, everything a congregation does is part of its witness; if it treats commercial activity in an instrumental way, it is sending a message about how it regards business, staff and profit. Such a message is at best dualist, because it sees spiritual endeavour as superior to material, and at worst cynical, because it is using people's labour, or even demeaning, because it is regarding the work of some as of less account than the efforts of others. So the congregation will almost inevitably find itself moving towards the exemplary model, enthusiastically or reluctantly. But if it embraces the exemplary approach, and it has the capacity to oversee such a venture, the rewards are much more than just financial.

Many congregations cultivate an attitude of studious observation: priding themselves on protest, advocacy and calling on who knows who to change who knows what. But a successful and exemplary business makes it possible to seek more than that. It creates the opportunity to do several things most churches can't dream of doing. Where many are content to survive, such a congregation can thrive, and model what a healthy, sustainable, just, ecological organization might look like, in its relations with God, one another and the created world, in its pattern of work and ministry and mission, prayer and play. If it flourishes, others may invite it to come alongside them and inspire them to combine commerce with congregational life. It can be part of reinvigorating the wider church from a disempowered state of complaint, resentment, impoverishment and nostalgia to a vibrant condition of action, confidence, generosity and healthy pride.

Just as within every congregation there are voices sceptical about the faithfulness of ministry expenditure, and demanding all resources be put towards mission, so in every congregational business similar voices will regard exemplary business as inadequate unless it adopts what I have called the social approach. The social approach wants every employee to be an ex-offender, or formerly homeless; wants every raw material to be locally sourced; and wants all wages and benefits to be the best in the sector. Advocates of the social approach long for the day when a stranger might wander in and see the activity of the business in its different dimensions, and its integration with the regular ministry of the congregation in worship, fellowship, education and pastoral care, and ask, 'This kingdom you speak of – this communion, this turning of society into community, this freedom and flourishing beyond market and state, this company of grace – what does it look like?' And those advocates could then turn around, and sweep their hand over every aspect of the community's life together, and say, gently but truly: 'It looks like this.'

It goes without saying that the more the exemplary approach looks and feels like the social approach, the better in almost every way. But an honest conversation needs to be had about the principal aim of the enterprise. If the intention is to fund a mission of which the congregation is already rightly proud, which is flourishing in every way besides mustering sufficient funds, then there's nothing to apologize for in the exemplary approach. If, however, there is no such flourishing mission, and/or if there is no significant imperative to raise funds to sustain it, then the social approach may become that outstanding, ideal form of mission. But the important recognition is that the social approach is mission, wholly or largely evaluated by its positive impact on those beyond the congregation, whereas the exemplary approach is better thought of as ministry – building up the congregation and making it more fit for mission. It's not that the exemplary approach is an inadequate or too-worldly version of the social approach; they are different things, designed for different ends. In the first, the profit is primary, the impact secondary; in the second, the impact is primary, the profit secondary. There can be excellent examples of both: but they are very seldom if ever successfully combined in the same project.

And this is where the balanced approach comes in as a variant of the social approach. As I have pointed out, most organizations find it next to impossible to make a genuine profit at the same time as making space to broaden their hiring policies and prioritize training and support for vulnerable employment groups. But before that sounds like a lack of faith or aspiration, it's helpful to recognize that harmonizing such divergent goals is exactly what the congregation seeks to do in its ministry life all the time. Congregations invite those with disabilities to read a lesson in worship, or preside at Holy Communion, and invest in lapel microphones or flexible liturgical furniture as appropriate to accommodate various needs. Congregations ask a person with a conviction for fraud to lead a working party tidying the churchyard; they take for granted that a person who has little or no money to contribute to the collection is nonetheless an equal and honoured member of the flock and can attend the parish away weekend without paying the full cost. It is precisely to maintain these kinds of practices, which some might call radical but congregations come to assume are normal, that instrumental or exemplary enterprises are set up in the first place. The best role of a business is to support an already dynamic ministry and mission; not to substitute for one that is not already there.

The beatitudes of business

I have sought to dispel some of the unhelpful contrasts conventionally drawn between business and church, and show how a congregation can both sustain and renew its life by finding the right kind of business model to adopt. What congregations should be striving for is to unite efficiency and integrity. Efficiency is doing the thing right, to maximize profits and achieve goals; integrity is doing the right thing. It's not quite the hypostatic union – which holds Jesus to be fully human and fully divine – but it's nonetheless a conviction that business and charity may be pursued wholeheartedly alongside each other, where integrity refines efficiency, and efficiency earths integrity. When a church has drawn together commercial and charitable activities within or alongside its congregational life, it is becoming an institution with social and economic significance.

In 1925, Fredrick Lewis Donaldson preached a sermon at Westminster Abbey in which he referred to seven social sins. Mahatma Gandhi adopted this list and published it later the same year. Those sins are

- Wealth without work.
- Pleasure without conscience.
- Knowledge without character.
- Commerce without morality.
- Science without humanity.

- Religion without sacrifice.
- Politics without principle.

The list hasn't dated very much. Those who craft institutions with economic and social as well as congregational dimensions don't say to everyone else, 'This is how you're wrong', but say to themselves, 'We're going to make our boldest effort to do the right thing, and to do it right.'

Near the beginning of his ministry Jesus articulated eight expressions of what the kingdom of God entailed, known as the Beatitudes. The sentiments of his charter have been called the most important words spoken by the most important person that ever lived. In the spirit of that charter, I want to suggest eight expressions of what a healthy blend of charitable venture and commercial enterprise might entail, as an attempt to respond to the seven social sins. These Beatitudes are written not from the point of view of the leaders, the customers or the beneficiaries of the institution, but from that of its employees. What should it be like to work for a business? I suggest as follows.

Blessed are those who are needed, for they will find purpose in serving. For a congregation to set up a company is an act of humility, because it recognizes that if the church is to survive, let alone flourish, it needs the energy and skill of people who are not part of its congregation, and in many cases not Christians. The same is true of a congregation that sets up a charity to enlist help in advancing its mission. But there's a great power in saying 'I need you'. Most people thrive on being needed, and are longing to serve if it's in a worthy cause.

Blessed are those who are involved, for they will discover joy in teamwork. If we need to carry out a simple task to support the business or charity, we need to be told precisely what expectations are in order that we not be set up to fail. But if we've had some say in working out what makes a good event, then we feel an entirely different level of engagement, and we share the joy if it goes well. Like a football team that wins a game, at the end we high-five and know the wonder of the word 'together'.

Blessed are those who are noticed, for they will bring forth surprising gifts. Institutions often use the word 'inclusion', but what really matters is being *seen*. Being seen means others perceiving our real talents, which may not immediately be closely related to the task we've been hired to fulfil. But every team grows from 'What must this team achieve?' to 'What can only this team achieve?' That's the journey from good to great.

Blessed are those who are rewarded, for they will create a culture of gratitude. This means paying people healthy wages, so their lives become sustainable, just as the organization becomes sustainable. It's a statement that if an institution is about promoting beauty, truth and goodness externally then these things must also be present internally. If we each know people have gone the extra mile for us, we're motivated to go the extra mile for others.

Blessed are those who are listened to, for they will foster a love of learning. W. Deen Muhammad, leader of the American Society of Muslims, used to say, 'We exist for two things: knowledge and mercy.' When things go well, we ask one another, 'What was the secret?' When they go badly, we say, 'What would we do differently?' If you have the courage to ask someone a question you don't already know the answer to, you're telling that person they matter, and that you need them to become a better person yourself.

Blessed are those who are given space to grow, for they will find out what they were put on this earth to be. It's always a great question to ask someone, 'How have you grown in the last year?' An organization that just tells people what to do is using them as servants or worse. An organization that's helping people reach their potential is genuinely enjoying them. To grow means to surprise others and yourself. Growth is the reward for giving people space to discover who they really are.

Blessed are those who are challenged, for they will reveal what they're really made of. To be challenged means to be placed in situations where the adrenalin runs faster because we've never done it before, but also to be held accountable for standards below which we shouldn't fall. When we say 'Bring your A game to work', we're saying if you want to learn, discover, grow and find purpose, you're not going to do it by taking the easy option.

Blessed are those who are trusted, for they will become leaders themselves. When Christopher Wren walked unrecognized among the craftsmen working on St Paul's Cathedral, he asked one labourer, 'What are you doing?' and the workman replied, 'I'm cutting stone.' Later he asked another the same question, and the man said, 'I'm building the house of God.' If you're trusted, you come to realize this is yours as much as it's anybody's. You've gone from being an employee to being a leader yourself.

When Jesus uttered the Beatitudes he was saying to his disciples, 'It's not enough to have faith; you have to make your life and the life of your community a living example of what the Holy Spirit can do.'[6] The grave of Christopher Wren lies in the crypt of St Paul's Cathedral. There's no great towering memorial. Only these words: 'If you are searching for his monument, look around.' That is the reward for those who create institutions that integrate charitable, commercial and congregational dimensions: their successors can say, 'If you are searching for their monument, look around.'

Kingdom business

I haven't discussed the secrets of what makes a profitable business, on which the available literature is vast, or which types of goods or services make the best fit for congregations to develop, which is a matter for local expertise, research and judgement.

Instead, I want to learn the lessons of the parable of the shrewd manager explored in my introduction, that generosity is the best investment, happiness lies in learning to love the things God gives in plenty, and business is primarily a matter of making friends. How does a congregation strike the right balance and foster business that celebrates and announces the kingdom, rather than one that obscures or diminishes the kingdom?

I'm going to suggest four avenues of enquiry that a congregation might pursue as it seeks to evaluate whether to proceed with a commercial venture, and whether to continue with one in its existing form or to change it wholly or partly.

The first is to have a clear answer to the question, 'What counts as success?' Assuming we are talking about an exemplary business – the second approach described above – the criteria must be sufficiently narrow to be achievable, yet adequately broad to be worth achieving. They must include generating enough profit to sustain the ministry and mission of the church, in such respects as existing forms of income, like congregational giving, are insufficient. But they may also include questions such as:

- Is this enterprise bringing a whole new range of people into face-to-face relationship with the church and leaving them with positive impressions and experiences?
- Is the process of employment enriching the congregation by rubbing shoulders with people who are happy to work for a church but would previously have been unlikely ever to attend one?
- Are we together unobtrusively changing the whole notion of church if we are celebrating the ministry of the Muslim finance head or the Jewish HR manager, and setting their contribution alongside the church treasurer or the occasional attender at the midweek service?

Such questions go way beyond asking if this church is now able to pay its bills. They recognize that a commercial enterprise has the potential to revolutionize a congregation for good.

The polarization between hard-nosed business success and sentimental failure is exposed as a false one. A commercial venture will inevitably involve, affect and benefit more people than originally envisaged. To establish such a project is to take a step of faith that those encounters will be beneficial ones. Which takes us into the second area of enquiry: does the church really believe it is called to an incarnate ministry, addressing the pragmatics of earning a living, sustaining employment, addressing pensions and sick benefits, transacting monetary exchanges, and making difficult decisions that can disappoint some and even hurt others? Jesus was a carpenter's son; Paul was a tentmaker. Even the central figures of the Christian faith had to experience the reality of making money to live on, and presumably they found a way to make the practice a blessing. It may be helpful to recognize that conventional congregational stewardship is in practice an instrumental approach: the church takes no responsibility for how the money donated has originally been raised – whether by fraud or extortion or stealing or sharp practice or wholesome non-exploitative honest wage for honest work. Is not congregational enterprise, in full public view, more likely to be the way of integrity? Is not a scheme like this, in which a whole array of members can take appropriate roles, potentially an opportunity to witness like never before? Here is a living example of how the challenges of discipleship and daily life may be understood, pondered and engaged. It is a living statement that salvation is not an escape from worldly reality but living God's future in the midst of present circumstances. Such an enterprise can be a living sacrament of hope in such a way.

This opens a third area of exploration: is the business making the congregation more honest – or less? There's no doubt that professionalism and success take a bit of getting used to in a country that has seldom been in the habit of associating such terms with the word 'church'. There's a way in which professionalism and success can keep a congregation honest because they dismantle the myth that the church lives on air; and they require and inspire everyone to maintain strong organizational standards about everything they do. But there's also a way in which commercial profits can keep a congregation dishonest because they can make it possible to have a flourishing church life without the congregation paying all the bills, which is a luxury few churches can comprehend. Nonetheless, it's possible to have commercial activities and administrative practices that deepen and embody a congregation's understanding of the kingdom, rather than conflict with or confuse it. Business brings into a church's life, as customers and staff, a myriad of people who otherwise might not come near, and a diversity of identity that's dynamic and energizing. By serving people and creating a staff team, a congregation learns what love and justice and flourishing mean when translated into economic decisions and regular habits of trade and employment. If the church wants to pay good wages, it has to make sacrifices elsewhere; if it wants to sell fair trade lines, it has to ensure they're attractive; if it wants to give disadvantaged people a step on the employment ladder, it needs to give them appropriate support. It's seldom easy, but the rewards go far beyond financial stability.

Finally comes the question that absorbs all the other questions. Is this what the kingdom looks like? Subsequent chapters explore how culture and compassion reflect and embody the kingdom; but these don't come as great surprises. For a truly holistic account, daily encounter with the incarnate reality of how people live and sustain their lives, and collective endeavour to keep a community going not with dramatic gifts but with careful, humble acts of common purpose is a beautiful yet pragmatic epiphany of craft and grace. It may not be necessary, possible or desirable for every congregation, but it could be the single most dynamic step in revitalizing the church for a future that's bigger than the past.

Notes

1 Kevin Hargaden, *Theological Ethics in a Neoliberal Age: Confronting the Christian Problem with Wealth* (Eugene, OR: Cascade,

2018), p. 26 (italics original). What Hargaden means by neoliberalism is very similar to what we saw John Milbank and Adrian Pabst meant by liberalism in Chapter 1.

2 Hargaden, p. 26.

3 Hargaden, p. 29, quoting Martin Luther, 'The Large Catechism', in *Triglot Concordia: The Symbolical Books of the Evangelical Lutheran Church* (St Louis: Concordia, 1921), pp. 565–773. Hargaden is also drawing on Philip Goodchild, *Theology of Money* (London: SCM Press, 2007).

4 The balanced approach is adapted from Paul Cheng and Joe Ludlow, 'The 3 Models of Social Enterprise: Creating Social Impact through Trading Activities' (Venturesome, *The Charities Aid Foundation*, 2008), https://community-wealth.org/sites/clone.community-wealth.org/files/downloads/article-cheng-ludlow.pdf.

5 'The Three Models of Social Enterprises: Creating Social Impact through Trading Activities: Part 2' (Venturesome, The Charities Aid Foundation, p. 11, July 2008), www.cafonline.org/docs/default-source/about-us-publications/venturesome3modelsofsocialenterprisepart2.pdf?sfvrsn=1315f440_3.

6 Stanley Hauerwas rightly points out that the Beatitudes of Matthew 5 are not recommendations about how to be happy. Matthew is telling us that, if you follow Jesus, this is how you will end up. Stanley Hauerwas, *Matthew* (Grand Rapids: Brazos, 2006), pp. 60–5. I am using the Beatitudes analogously here, appealing to an aspirational understanding of business as part of discipleship, ministry and mission.

4

Entertaining Angels Unawares:
It is More Blessed to Receive

In this chapter I make three moves. The first is to try to dismantle the assumption that church and charity are both fundamentally personal matters, which shouldn't get entangled with social or political consequences or commitments. The second is to scrutinize conventional notions of charity, which can easily do more harm than good. The third is to articulate what good charity means, and how that may best relate to congregational life. I end the chapter with a meditation on one particular social issue, and how the gospel engages it.

The personal is the political

In the late 1960s, the second wave of the feminist movement started to use the phrase 'the personal is political'. What the phrase meant was that many of the choices that women made, or were denied the opportunity to make, were not simply personal choices but together constituted the heart of the way politics needed to be reimagined and reconfigured. Politics was fundamentally tangled up in the personal, and the personal was what the tangle of politics was all about. Issues of violence against women, of sexual health, of salary and working conditions, of the availability of affordable and high-quality day care, and of the removal of impossible beauty standards from one's life, were not private, personal questions. On the contrary, they were exactly what politics was about. The feminist movement taught many other minority and under-represented groups that the key to social change was to expose and manifest the public significance of hitherto hidden and private personal struggles and sufferings. Such an insight has become a commonplace among activists today, for example in the environmental movement. We are all encouraged to recognize that the future well-being of the planet doesn't just lie in international agreements made in Rio, Kyoto and Copenhagen, but just as much in our decision to recycle our daily newspaper, ride a bike to work and purchase locally grown vegetables.

The phrase 'the personal is the political' may have been invented in the 1960s, but the idea is not new. The idea is at the heart of the Passion narrative. The power of the story of Jesus' suffering and death is that it is both an account of the greatest political tragedy in history, the death of the son of God, and a display of the most profound and intimate personal and interpersonal interactions and betrayals. That's the whole point. It's never just about God, and it's never just about us. Jesus goes to the cross because we put him there, but also because God somehow chose to let him go there. The agony of the story is not just that Jesus gives his life to save the whole world, but that he lays down his life for his friends. It is personal and political, political and personal, all at the same time, and you can never disentangle the one from the other.

When Judas kisses Jesus in the Garden of Gethsemane, his kiss is the most intimate, ironic form of betrayal. The act of love becomes the act of exposure. But that kiss is the most political thing Judas does in the whole story. Judas uses his personal knowledge of Jesus and his purposes and whereabouts and turns that knowledge into political power by bringing a movement that challenged the Roman and Jewish status quo to an abrupt and violent end. Then, by the charcoal fire, Peter's personal need for warmth and his very human fear of being recognized, and perhaps executed, become a political changing of sides. A servant girl says, 'You were with the Galilean', and in the process makes the motley crew of disciples sound more like a political party. When Peter denies it, he isn't just betraying his closest friend, he's putting his weight behind the Roman and Sadduccean and Herodian domination of Galilee and Jerusalem. Again, when Pontius Pilate sits on the judgement seat, we see apparently the most political moment of all. Pilate asks if Jesus is the King of the Jews; he is in the habit of releasing one prisoner to the crowd. These are patently political dimensions of the story. But suddenly it gets very personal. Pilate's wife appears and her message arrives at this most political moment with an extraordinarily personal touch: 'I can't sleep, darling, I've had a terrible dream, it's been upsetting me all day. I've been dreaming about another man, not you. And the man I've been dreaming about is the man standing half naked in front of you right now. Don't kill him, please, whatever you do.' It makes one wonder, did Pilate have Jesus executed out of realpolitik, or out of jealousy – for political reasons, or personal ones? Most poignantly, when Jesus dies on the cross, he calls out 'My God, my God, why have you forsaken me?' Some assume he's calling for Elijah, and placing himself in the religious and political history of Israel's prophets, while others assume he's thirsty and take his cry in a more personal way by offering him a drink on the end of a stick. Moments later, the centurion looks on Jesus' dead body and concludes, 'This man was God's son', which sounds like a personal statement of affirmation or even faith, but when one realizes this was a Roman soldier and his emperor claimed the title Son of God it becomes evident it's not just a personal statement but a deeply political one.

To be a Christian means to follow Jesus' path to the cross in the hope of sharing with him in his resurrection. The Passion narrative gives us every indication that if we follow Jesus we can expect some public acclaim but eventual rejection. We can be weighed down like the disciples by human needs like sleepiness in the garden and shivering cold by the charcoal fire. But we can also be called to the most transcendent gestures, like Simon carrying Jesus' cross and Joseph stepping out of the shadows to offer a tomb. What we can't do is try to seal off parts of our lives. We can't say 'This part is personal', and deny that it has any political significance. We can't say 'That part is political', and thereby suppose it's immune from the call to discipleship. The difference between the personal and the political is meaningless to God. God sees it all. God knows it all. God wants it all.

Who do you eat with? What groceries do you buy? Who do you sit next to in church? Which route, and what method of transport, do you take to work? What literature do you read? Who do you pray for? These intensely personal things constitute some of the most politically significant statements of our lives. Who do you know that came to this country in search of a better job? Who do you know that has had an unexpected and unplanned pregnancy? Who do you know whose father died in a war no one can remember the need for? These are supposed to be political questions; but issues are only generalizations about people. The political is intensely personal, when we really allow ourselves to see it. In the first Holy Week, Peter, Judas, Simon of Cyrene, Mary Magdalene and Joseph of Arimathea discovered that their most personal friendships, choices and loves turned out to be the most political and dynamic dimensions of their lives. Discipleship requires each of us to make the same discovery.

All of which highlights that there's no church or charity that isn't political and personal at the same time. Politics is revealed in the most personal choices and relationships of our lives. The biggest act of charity disciples do isn't the way they give away their money, it's with whom they choose to be in relationship. The biggest political act disciples perform is not how they cast their vote, but how they let the worship and witness of their church form their character. Likewise, there's no artificial distinction between church and charity. The first social action of the church is to be the church. That's by no means the church's only social action, but it's a recognition that being church is a political and social act of the first importance even before it issues in other forms of action. Charity is the explicit public declaration and demonstration of who the church thinks it is and whom it believes it is called to be with.

What's wrong with charity

In a blistering attack on ideas of charity that were the norm in the 1890s, and are still widely held today, Oscar Wilde makes a series of crisp observations that bear close attention more than 120 years after they were written.[1] Dismissing the conventional compassion of his and our age, Wilde points out that most people are drawn to charity, but in a way that does no good. He maintains the 'majority of people spoil their lives by an unhealthy and exaggerated altruism'. They are surrounded by hideous poverty, ugliness and starvation, and are accordingly moved by 'admirable, though misdirected intentions' to remedy the evils around them. But what Wilde recognizes is that 'their remedies do not cure the disease: they merely prolong it. Indeed, their remedies are part of the disease.'

Wilde contends that most attempts at charity are misguided, and often result in shoring up an unjust situation that needs to be exposed, allowed to fail and replaced:

> Just as the worst slave-owners were those who were kind to their slaves, and so prevented the horror of the system being realised by those who suffered from it, and understood by those who contemplated it, so, in the present state of things in England, the people who do most harm are the people who try to do most good.

Wilde provocatively insists, 'Charity creates a multitude of sins' – not least that it degrades and demoralizes its objects. Wilde is relentless in his argument that conventional notions of virtue compound the problem and need to be denounced.

> The virtues of the poor may be readily admitted, and are much to be regretted. We are often told that the poor are grateful for charity. Some of them are, no doubt, but the best amongst the poor are never grateful. They are ungrateful, discontented, disobedient, and rebellious. They are quite right to be so. Charity they feel to be a ridiculously inadequate mode

of partial restitution, or a sentimental dole, usually accompanied by some impertinent attempt on the part of the sentimentalist to tyrannise over their private lives. Why should they be grateful for the crumbs that fall from the rich man's table? They should be seated at the board, and are beginning to know it. As for being discontented, a [person] who would not be discontented with such surroundings and such a low mode of life would be a perfect brute. Disobedience, in the eyes of anyone who has read history, is [humankind's] original virtue. It is through disobedience that progress has been made, through disobedience and through rebellion.

In similar vein, Wilde has no time for the well-worn distinction between the deserving and the undeserving poor. He is in no mood to hand out certificates to those of the poor that meet the wealthy's criteria for benevolence. 'Sometimes,' he says, 'the poor are praised for being thrifty.' But Wilde believes 'to recommend thrift to the poor is both grotesque and insulting'. He maintains that a town or country labourer who practises thrift is demonstrating an ability to live like a badly fed animal. Wilde would prefer that such people 'should either steal or go on the rates, which is considered by many to be a form of stealing'. He summarizes the alternatives like this: 'It is safer to beg than to take, but it is finer to take than to beg.' He would much rather people be 'ungrateful, unthrifty, discontented, and rebellious' – all of which are healthy forms of protest. He has little time for the so-called virtuous poor, whom he sees as objects of pity rather than admiration: 'They have made private terms with the enemy, and sold their birthright for very bad pottage. They must also be extraordinarily stupid.' Wilde doesn't understand why people who have no prospect of realizing 'some form of beautiful and intellectual life' should accept laws that protect private property: he sees it as almost incredible how a person 'whose life is marred and made hideous by such laws can possibly acquiesce in their continuance'.

Wilde does have good news for the poor: yet it doesn't lie simply in the redistribution of wealth or any change in the democratic

arrangements for elections, which in 1890 had a restricted fran-
chise, not least in that they excluded women altogether. Instead,
Wilde goes to the heart of what constitutes human flourishing,
and offers counsel on how best to foster it. He describes human
flourishing as the development of what he calls 'personality',
and he believes Jesus' purpose was to encourage the growth of
such personality. Seeking to gain property is largely a distraction
from this higher goal. This is Wilde's prescription:

> Jesus moved in a community that allowed the accumulation
> of private property just as ours does, and the gospel that he
> preached was not that in such a community it is an advantage
> for a [person] to live on scanty, unwholesome food, to wear
> ragged, unwholesome clothes, to sleep in horrid, unwhole-
> some dwellings, and a disadvantage for a [person] to live
> under healthy, pleasant, and decent conditions . . . What
> Jesus meant was this. He said to [humankind], 'You have a
> wonderful personality. Develop it. Be yourself. Don't imag-
> ine that your perfection lies in accumulating or possessing
> external things. Your affection is inside of you. If only you
> could realise that, you would not want to be rich. Ordinary
> riches can be stolen from a [person]. Real riches cannot. In
> the treasury-house of your soul, there are infinitely precious
> things, that may not be taken from you. And so, try to so
> shape your life that external things will not harm you . . .' It
> is to be noted that Jesus never says that impoverished people
> are necessarily good, or wealthy people necessarily bad. That
> would not have been true . . . There is only one class in the
> community that thinks more about money than the rich, and
> that is the poor. The poor can think of nothing else. That is
> the misery of being poor. What Jesus does say is that [human-
> kind] reaches [its] perfection, not through what [it] has, not
> even through what [it] does, but entirely through what [it] is.

In these excoriating words, Wilde articulates a formidable critique of notions of charity that still abide today. Altruism,
he argues, may often in origin be misguided, sentimental and

patronizing, and in outcome be counterproductive and pernicious. Trying to do good invariably serves the giver but seldom benefits the recipient. That generosity for which the rich are often applauded and that humility for which the poor are commended most often leaves the status quo unchallenged, and thus does more harm than good. Counsel given to the poor by the rich is generally grotesque and insulting. Seventy years before Paulo Freire, Wilde argues that the best thing those who are not poor can do is to make the poor aware of their paralysed consciousness, since 'no class is ever really conscious of its own suffering. They have to be told of it by other people, and they often entirely disbelieve them.' This was how the cause of abolition prevailed in the United States. Such agitators are indispensable, he believes, and the fate of the poor without them pitiful. For Wilde, 'The most tragic fact in the whole of the French Revolution is not that Marie Antoinette was killed for being a queen, but that the starved peasants of the Vendée voluntarily went out to die for the hideous cause of feudalism.' Yet the solution to poverty is not to give everyone a property portfolio. Property can be a burden as much as a blessing: it is at best only ever a means to an end. The key to flourishing is to see that we realize our potential not through what we have, not even through what we do, but entirely through what we are.

In characteristically radical terms, Wilde goes on to challenge the whole way charity is conventionally and almost universally founded on compassion, and on what he takes to be an inaccurate notion of unselfishness. These are the words with which he apparently undermines, but in fact releases, the potential of true charity.

> Selfishness is not living as one wishes to live, it is asking others to live as one wishes to live. And unselfishness is letting other people's lives alone, not interfering with them. Selfishness always aims at creating around it an absolute uniformity of type. Unselfishness recognises infinite variety of type as a delightful thing, accepts it, acquiesces in it,

enjoys it . . . A red rose is not selfish because it wants to be a red rose. It would be horribly selfish if it wanted all the other flowers in the garden to be both red and roses . . . Up to the present [humanity] has hardly cultivated sympathy at all. [It] has merely sympathy with pain, and sympathy with pain is not the highest form of sympathy. All sympathy is fine, but sympathy with suffering is the least fine mode. It is tainted with egotism. It is apt to become morbid. There is in it a certain element of terror for our own safety. We become afraid that we ourselves might be as the leper or as the blind, and that no [one] would have care of us. It is curiously limiting, too. One should sympathise with the entirety of life, not with life's sores and maladies merely, but with life's joy and beauty and energy and health and freedom. The wider sympathy is, of course, the more difficult. It requires more unselfishness. Anybody can sympathise with the sufferings of a friend, but it requires a very fine nature . . . to sympathise with a friend's success.

Wilde is proposing that charity be founded not on compassion or pity, nor even enlightened self-interest, and still less a patronizing desire to 'teach a man to fish', but on a genuine quest for true companionship. Now that would be something.[2]

Wider misgivings

Oscar Wilde's criticisms are profound. They're worth quoting because they offer not just reasons to evaluate charity carefully, but a possible alternative vision. Nonetheless, his scepticism about charity is shared by many inside and beyond the church. Misgivings about charity can be grouped into concerns about the purpose, methods and outcomes.

Concerns about the *purpose* begin with the general observation that charity tends to be about the heart more than the head; some would say about the egoist's desire to leave a mark rather than the altruist's lack of care about who gets the credit.

Charitable endeavours do not always begin from extensive research and close understanding about the issues they seek to address. They are not always mindful of the range of effects and side-effects an intervention might cause or trigger. They can be dominated by the needs and projections of the activist and donor and pay little regard to the actual circumstances of the recipient or beneficiary. They tend to run on a deficit model that focuses on what is lacking in the recipient and what is abundant in the activist or donor – and thus undermine the qualities in the beneficiary on which future well-being will depend. They can rely on emotional appeal, with the result that donors give out of compassion rather than wisdom, and sentimental causes benefit while more sophisticated needs miss out. Giving can be driven just as much by a company's desire to look good, or by individual donors' quests to find tax loopholes, as from genuine concern about issues and people; still less to restore true relationship among people.

As to the *methods*, these concerns are in many cases closely related to the motivations. The words 'volunteer' and 'amateur' have very positive origins, but can be easily associated with things not being done with care and professionalism. A charity that is shaped largely or wholly by the activist's or donor's passionate perception of desperate crisis or crying tragedy is unlikely to pay careful attention to what other organizations are doing, and may have been doing for a long time, slow to learn lessons that others have gleaned, and reluctant to form partnerships to maximize effectiveness. The fact that there are around 200,000 registered charities in the UK and 200 homeless charities in London alone speaks of the sector's notorious tendencies to multiplication and duplication. Relatively few charities have, on their boards, significant representation from the groups they seek to serve: thus decisions are too often taken that reflect the presuppositions of the activist and donor rather than the genuine vision of the beneficiary. Since charity is often focused on the desire to act, rather than the aspiration to change, impact assessments can be weak and accountability lines can be absent: there never seems time to review how things went last time in the eagerness to keep doing more. As to fundraising, there are always concerns about whether charities abide by best practice in presenting their case and respecting donors; and always the danger that major donors or corporations will constrain the way their money is spent. When a charity's income is over-dependent on a small number of sources it is open to manipulation. Meanwhile, there is often suspicion of Christian charities that their real aim is the dissemination of the faith rather than the autonomous well-being of the beneficiary.

When it comes to outcomes, which is Oscar Wilde's main concern, the passionate desire to change the world can often result in the wrong kind of change. An abiding concern for many is that charities simply let governments off the hook by conducting work that should come out of the public purse. Another frequent worry is that charities foster a co-dependent culture where their clients become habituated to using their services and the charities themselves need the clients to justify their existence. Charities can become part of a system: the frequent user can learn to play such a system, while the genuinely needy can become lost within it.

Such misgivings drive clarity about motivations, methods and outcomes. They also encourage vigilance about spotting the moment when a goodwill gesture becomes an institutional programme.[3]

Changing life, Changing lives

Keeping Wilde's vivid critique and these wider misgivings in mind, it's time to review what anyone, church or beyond, might be trying to do through charitable or other benevolent action. Since these more fundamental questions are too seldom asked, it could be helpful to explore them before making further proposals. Rather than draw up categories and select between them, it may be most illuminating to begin with perhaps the most obvious kind of charitable endeavour – feeding the hungry – and then assess what makes it more or less suitable as an aspiration.

If there are 7.6 billion people in the world, then around 815 million, or just over one in ten, is suffering from chronic undernourishment. Meanwhile, the number of people affected each year by hydrological, meteorological, climatological, geophysical or biological disasters (floods, storms, droughts, earthquakes and diseases) is around 400 million. These numbers dwarf any other measurement of human need. One would therefore imagine that all charitable efforts would be directed to overseas development aid or humanitarian relief unless there were pressing reasons to the contrary.

In fact only 10 per cent of UK charitable giving goes to overseas aid and disaster relief, and only 19 per cent of adults who give to charity regularly give to such causes. There are a number of drawbacks to such charities. It is very difficult for the donor to see the results of their support. It is just as difficult for a supporter to play any significant role in the charity besides giving money and encouraging others to do so. There is almost no prospect of face-to-face encounter between supporters and beneficiaries; it requires a bureaucratic system of wise distribution, dependent on professional staff and local partners on the ground in development regions or disaster zones: there is nothing a volunteer can usefully do. There are numerous pitfalls in regard to the conduct of professional staff, the durability and standards of local partners, issues of waste, maldistribution and endemic corruption in local cultures, and the perpetual balance between humanitarian relief and political agitation in richer and poorer nations that seeks to interrupt the perpetuation of circumstances that make populations so vulnerable. In a larger perspective, seeing people or nations only as the recipient of charity can be humiliating and degrading in the way Wilde identifies.

Scrutinizing such drawbacks reveals a good deal about what makes for good charity. Good charity sees the donor as more than just a source of money and the recipient as more than simply a needy cause. Good charity cares not just for the beneficiary's survival, but for their dignity, well-being, network of relationships, ability to earn a living, education, training, health and general flourishing, not least their ability to be a benefactor to others.

Good charity recognizes not only the powerlessness of the recipient to bring about the changes in their life they long to see but also the powerlessness of the donor to feel that they are enhancing people's capacity and helping them realize their potential, rather than compounding the problem by perpetuating humiliation or cultivating dependency. Good charity recognizes that human problems are more often about isolation and the fragility of relationships than about limitation and the shortage of materials, and that efforts to overcome limitation by supplying materials or technology can end up increasing isolation by undermining networks of relationship. Good charity does not seek to make the recipient more like the donor, but catalyses a journey in which both donor and recipient may grow and flourish, ideally but not always through coming to know, respect and learn from each other.

And this is why Oscar Wilde's swingeing criticism of conventional well-meaning benevolence is so important. He is well aware of the familiar motivations of guilt, self-importance, duty, evangelism and pity that pervade the charitable scene, then and now. But beyond these he identifies one rather more subtle desire. Consider again these words:

> Selfishness is not living as one wishes to live, it is asking others to live as one wishes to live. And unselfishness is letting other people's lives alone, not interfering with them. Selfishness always aims at creating around it an absolute uniformity of type. Unselfishness recognizes infinite variety of type as a delightful thing, accepts it, acquiesces in it, enjoys it.

What Wilde puts his finger on is the narcissistic impulse to recreate the world in the image of ourselves. This impulse is then presented as charity. In fact, anything significantly different from ourselves is problematic – we struggle with the successes of others as much as we do their failures. Here is Wilde's crucial sentence: 'One should sympathise with the entirety of life, not with life's sores and maladies merely, but with life's joy and beauty and energy and health and freedom.' One might almost say, love keeps no score of wrongs, but rejoices in the good. Charity is not a foul-weather friend that thrives on another's hardship, nor a rescuer that cannot see what a person is, only what they can become with assistance that is provided on the rescuer's terms. Charity seeks 'life's joy and beauty and energy and health and freedom', yet chooses not to seek such things alone, but in the company of those for whom others might suppose such things were out of reach.

This is the secret of good charity: not to carry around solutions and hunt for those with suitable problems from whom you may derive pleasure in supplying a fix; not to civilize the world by making it an image of yourself; not to subcontract your guilt and pay off the distressing calls of need from your gate with a regular retainer to one who will venture where you disdain to go; not to immerse yourself in others' pain so as to feel better about your shortcomings or hardships; but to allow your life to be harnessed to those whose talent you believe in but have not yet seen, whose potential is limitless but you have not yet witnessed, whose joy is elusive but you long to share, whose grasp of beauty will transform yours, and whose freedom, once attained, will make your choices seem tawdry and limited. This is what it means to say it is better to receive than to give. The world's problem is not that there are too many poor and the wealthy should give; it's that the joy in life is creativity, relationship and growth, and the poor are poor to the extent that they don't have outlets for such things, and charity means creating and becoming outlets for such things. Charity requires a step of faith: but that faith is not that you have a problem to which I must be able to find a solution; it's that you have a pearl inside you and by steadiness, durability, solidarity, trustworthiness, encouragement and companionship, I must be able to help you bring that pearl into the glowing sunshine to be beheld in all its glory.

How charity renews the church

Most mission is about individuals encountering God in the world beyond the church in unsystematic and often unanticipated ways through personal encounter with the stranger. There is no reason or need to structure or rationalize such encounters. There is no necessity to take away their spontaneity or ingenuousness. No effort to organize charitable endeavours or mission initiatives should diminish or discredit the priority and simplicity of authentic human encounter.

We have seen that there is good reason to turn the need for sustainable income into a concerted venture into commercial life. In just the same way, there are appropriate motives for organizing outreach initiatives into a specific legally constituted charity. These include tax advantages in gift aid, VAT and business rates. The structural aspects are about creating an organization that people can participate in, that grant-making bodies, benefactors and sometimes statutory bodies can fund, and that auditors and other agents for accountability can scrutinize – without getting tangled up in the life of the congregation. This has many dimensions. It means that if the circumstances of the congregation change, the charity can continue largely unaffected. Accounts are kept entirely separately, and the venture is recognized as having its own identity, separate from but largely in accord with the purposes of the church. It anticipates a time when the congregation and the charity may become entirely separate, in premises, identity, purpose, governance and personnel. It means that a person who is a member of another congregation can work or volunteer for the charity without appearing to change their loyalties, or donate to the charity without that becoming confused with their tithe to their own church. It means a person of another faith or of no professed faith can gladly work for, volunteer with or donate to the charity without feeling compromised by becoming regarded as an honorary congregation member. Likewise, a statutory authority, grant-maker or company social or employees' fund may exclude donations to churches but may be quite content to contribute to an independent charity. Moreover, the beneficiary of the initiative may be more comfortable being brought into the life of a charity or a particular one or two of its employees or volunteers than being embraced by a congregation. Together this clear water between a congregation and a charity makes it helpfully evident what the charity does that only a charity can do, and what the congregation does that only a congregation can do, without preventing individuals being involved in some capacity in both at the same time.

All of which is not to say that the transition is always easy or beneficial. It's not just that the process of becoming a charity can be demanding, complex and protracted. The requirement that all activities be charitable is too rigorous for many. Rules around trusteeship and campaigning activities may keep the charity focused on good operation and core activities. But the real issue for a small charity is the weight of administration, the heavy responsibility and the skills required to keep accounts, submit returns and embody good governance. In the process, the hand-to-mouth, happy-go-lucky character of a voluntary initiative can be inhibited, and the enjoyment much reduced. People may say, 'We're not a family any more', and they're often right, because a family has a certain exclusivity, non-transparency, hierarchy, conflict of interest and familiarity that's explicitly ruled out by a charitable structure, and while this is usually a very good thing, there's no doubt there can be genuine losses too.

For all these reasons, the decision on whether to establish a formal charity needs to be a local and circumstantial one. But the overall ethos has to be the one provoked by Oscar Wilde and described above as the transformation of a burden into a gift. Charity, or compassionate outreach, is not a weighty duty a congregation takes on because it feels guilty about the plight of those less fortunate than itself. It's a glad response to the angels God is sending the congregation's way and a decision to create and resource a specialized form of encounter with them. Such an encounter is about the congregation making new discoveries in faith and the theoretical beneficiaries finding truer living, greater hope and fuller expression for their creativity and talents. It is the attitude of expectation and the mutual desire to learn and grow that preserves such an initiative from patronizing interference reinforcing inequality. Such a venture does not drain a church of energy and resources: it renews a congregation through the energy and challenge of people on whom many, perhaps most, communities would customarily turn their back.

Three kinds of homelessness

I want to finish with a scriptural engagement that points to renewal around the issue I most often encounter. I offer this meditation in an attempt to model the kind of understanding provoked by Wilde and arising from the reflections of this chapter.

To be street homeless – to be a person who sleeps outside – is to face many challenges every day. The day probably begins early: the patch on which you're sleeping is likely to be needed as an access door, or your presence is challenged by a park attendant or security guard. Immediately you have to work out where to put your things, how to source some breakfast, where to charge your phone. Then the day begins in earnest. It's largely spent seeking to improve your situation, in the short term by gaining some income by doing some casual work, or in some cases begging, and in the long term by seeking to address your health needs, any other bureaucratic obstacles, and ideally making yourself more ready for regular work and finding some more sustainable accommodation. In the process you build up a network of relationships, with places you can get cardboard to sleep on, a sausage to chew on, hot water for tea, and space to leave your belongings; maybe there's a support worker who can assist you, another homeless person you can talk to, or an agency that will give you a chance to wash, do laundry, find nutritious food and human company.

People become homeless for all sorts of reasons; people remain homeless for a bunch more; people sometimes become homeless again after a more stable season; and the majority of people who are homeless find a way to exist that doesn't involve sleeping outside. But every category of homelessness is characterized by one common feature: shame. Shame, because you're without most of the sources of dignity and prestige our culture prizes: you have no home and therefore no castle; your clothes are rough and unstylish; you face daily humiliation by having to ask others for food, money, respect, assistance, eye contact; you risk constant judgement that you have brought this situation about through your own shortcomings; you have little security, few if any friends, little trust; a very small foundation on which to build a better future. All of us know what it feels like to be embarrassed, humiliated, exposed, judged, rejected, crushed – it's what we strive to avoid with all our hearts. But to be homeless is not just to feel these things – it's to feel them all the time.

We can get a particular perspective on homelessness if we consider the parable of the great banquet in Luke 14. The parable comes in four scenes. In scene one, a man invites the great and the good to a grand dinner and begins to make preparations. The story takes for granted that everyone wants to come to that dinner; why might anyone possibly say no? In scene two, the dinner is served and a servant duly goes to collect the guests. But here comes the shock: one guest says he needs to inspect some land, another says he's bought ten oxen, a third says he's just got married. Now it would be easy to say, 'How unfortunate, it's disappointing when you want your friends to come over and it turns out they're all busy.' But that would be to miss the point. In the first place, these people have already promised to come, and make no effort to say otherwise until the food is already prepared. In the second place, they're all offering excuses about things they would have been aware of well in advance. In the third place, their excuses are phrased in such a way as to cause maximum offence: the field is something that could obviously have waited, the oxen is a huge investment but one that requires meticulous calculation to match each pair in strength and size, and thus not something likely to be done in one evening, while the third is a crude and culturally inexcusable statement that the invitee is so taken up with the pleasures of the flesh that he has no regard for his host's hospitality.

The result is that the host is utterly humiliated. He could be angry, vengeful, bitter and vindictive. Many of us are, when the shroud of shame falls upon us and the light of dignity is removed from us. Whatever their motives, the guests have set out to cause wholesale humiliation and they've succeeded. But the host doesn't internalize the embarrassment or turn shame into anger. In scene three, he improvises and says, 'Why don't we give the food to someone who wants it? Why don't we turn a formal function into a playful party?' He instructs his servant to go around the town inviting those who would never normally be invited to any such gathering because, whether through their social or their physical condition, they know what it means to experience perpetual shame. In other words, in the heat of his shame, he chose to share what he had with those who knew shame better than he did. But it turns out that even when the shamed of the town are invited there are still seats left at the table. This tells us just how many of the original guests, beyond the three whose excuses are recorded, must have turned the host down. So in scene four the host tells the slaves to go beyond the town limits and into the countryside and find the ultra-shamed, that is to say, whoever is so ostracized that they're cast out from the town altogether.

Before making a connection to a congregation's own context it's important to see how this anticipates the story of Christ's Passion. Jesus is first tried among those whom one might expect to welcome his ministry. He's then paraded through the streets and lanes of Jerusalem and is exposed to humiliation and scorn. Finally, he's taken outside the city to the highways and byways and is put to death by the most shameful method known to the ancient world. But he doesn't internalize that shame. Instead he expresses forgiveness to his persecutors and in due course through his resurrection he turns that shame into grace. The cruelty and injustice of his tormentors he turns into hospitality and hope. The heart of the banquet story is the same as the heart of the gospel: shame and loss become grace and joy.

Now we may examine a congregation's context and reflect on three kinds of homelessness. The first is the plight of the person whose life has got into such a crisis, whose relationships are so fragile or non-existent, whose legal rights are so inadequate, and whose options are so exhausted that they experience the daily shame of being regarded as shiftless, pitiful and a lost cause.

The second is the members of the congregation's own home-lessness. Many are searching; some are isolated; others pine for belonging, relationship, home, acceptance, or an end to prejudice, exposure, failure, humiliation or scorn. If you ask people, 'Why do you like spending time with homeless people?' and you really want to wait for a reply, the answer almost always is, 'Because it helps me recognize and understand and find companionship in my own homelessness.' It's the same journey from shame to grace.

But there's a third kind of homelessness – and that's what we get a glimpse of in the parable. Jesus is saying, then and now, 'I have no home but yours. Yours is the heart where I belong. Yours is the home I long to enter. Yours is the life I long to resur-rect. Yours are the burdens I long to share.' And the door is con-tinually closed, or slammed in his face. That is the shame of God, not just on the cross, but today, every day, every minute, from those from whom we might most expect there to be a welcome.

The homelessness of the streets, the homelessness of ourselves, the homelessness of God. There's a moment when these three kinds of homelessness come together. And that's at the Eucharist, where Gentiles celebrate that God's invitation went not just to God's own people the Jews but to those who were in the highways and byways; the Eucharist, in which the rejected of the world, the failures of our lives and the broken heart of God meet; the Eucharist, in which the shroud of shame is lifted and the banquet of grace begins; where a formal function becomes a playful party, and injustice, ignominy and isolation are transformed into joy.

The promise of charity is that by sustained attention to one group of excluded or challenged people, members of a congre-gation will find the ordinary practices of their lives transformed into such a Eucharist. This is how compassion renews the church.

Notes

1 O. Wilde, 'The Soul of Man Under Socialism' (1891), retrieved from www.marxists.org/reference/archive/wilde-oscar/soul-man/.

2 Two books that make similar points to Oscar Wilde from a secular, US perspective are Anand Giridharadas, *Winners Take All: The Elite Charade of Changing the World* (New York: Knopf, 2018), and Rob Reich, *Just Giving: How Philanthropy is Failing Democracy and How it Can Do Better* (Princeton: Princeton University Press, 2018). Giridharadas sees the American philanthropic system as a culture that invites society's biggest winners to tell the rest what they are doing wrong. The tax system enables the rich to keep their often ill-gotten gains while flattering them for money and advice. Meanwhile, Trump is the *reductio ad absurdum* of a culture that tasks elites with reforming the very systems that have made them. I'm grateful to Will Morris for directing me to this dialogue.

3 Among a wide range of publications that share many of these concerns about global charity, two of the most helpful are Thomas Dichter, *Despite Good Intentions: Why Development Assistance to the Third World has Failed* (Boston: University of Massachusetts Press, 2003), and Robert D. Lupton, *Toxic Charity: How Churches and Charities Hurt Those They Help, and How to Reverse It* (San Francisco: HarperOne, 2012). Stanley Hauerwas summarizes these critiques as follows.

There are four primary reasons given for the failure of aid to poorer countries. First and foremost, aid is said not to work because the aid given was not effectively planned. Money was simply thrown at a problem with little idea of how the money could be best used to make a positive response to a definite need. As a result, the aid did not get to the people that actually need it but instead was virtually stolen by those in power. Secondly it is argued that even when aid is more carefully planned it does not achieve its objectives because aid is inherently a negative process. Aid creates a dependency in those who receive the aid that cannot easily be rectified. Third aid simply is a bandage on a wound that is much deeper than aid can address. Aid, it is argued, simply cannot overcome the chronically unjust international economic systems. Globalization is but another name for capitalism in which those that have will continue to have and those who do not have can do little to counter the power of the 'haves.' Finally, it is argued that aid does not work because it was not designed to work. Indeed it is not even clear what it would mean for aid to work. The poor are poor for numerous reasons but the bottom line is the poor got left out of the development of advanced economies and there is little one can do to rectify that reality.

Stanley Hauerwas, 'How to Remember the Poor,' in *The Work of Theology* (Grand Rapids: Eerdmans 2015) 208–28.

5

Making our Hearts Sing:
Let All the People Praise Thee

In this chapter I explore two understandings of the term 'culture', one general and one specific, and propose that a renewed approach to the more specific understanding may lead to a healthy form of the more general understanding. I then offer a humble example of what culture can mean in renewing a congregation.

Culture in general

The two understandings to which I refer are, on the one hand, a sense of culture as all-pervading – a kind of adverb to the verb of human existence – and, on the other hand, a perception of culture as specifically associated with artefacts of achievement in the field of the arts, and the different, more refined and aspirational world they depict.

Let me start with culture in general. For H. Richard Niebuhr, culture is the 'artificial, secondary environment which [humankind] superimposes on the natural. It comprises language, habits, ideas, beliefs, customs, social organization, inherited artefacts, technical processes, and values.'[1] 'This world of culture – [humankind's] achievement – exists within the world of grace – God's Kingdom.'[2]

This anthropological understanding of culture is always social, never 'private'; likewise, social life is always cultural. Culture is human achievement – it's the designed and laborious work of humankind's mind and hands. Culture is not non-human efforts or actions of humans without intention of results or control of the process. It includes speech, education, tradition, myth, science, art, philosophy, government, law, rites, beliefs, inventions, technologies. No one can possess it without their own effort and achievement. It concerns what people have purposely wrought and can or ought to do. Culture refers to the made and intended world. It is a world of values, because people make and do things for a purpose and design them to serve a good – in most cases, a human good. What is thought of as good is what is good for humanity, although not always only humanity. There is no nature that can be known apart from culture.

Niebuhr draws no explicit line between culture and what we might call high culture – between the inevitable way humans adopt, adapt and digest the natural world and the ways they seek to identify, articulate and portray its most salient features. Whether material or immaterial, culture requires human goods to be realized in temporal and material form.

> The harmony and proportion, the form, order and rhythm, the meanings and ideas that [people] intuit and trace out as they confront nature, social events, and the world of dreams, these by infinite labour they must paint on wall or canvas, print on paper as systems of philosophy or science, outline in carved stone or cast in bronze, sing in ballad, ode, or symphony. Visions of order and justice, hopes of glory, must at the cost of much suffering be embodied in written laws, dramatic rites, structures of government, empires, ascetic lives.[3]

For upholders of culture, conservation of values is as much a concern as their realization. Buildings decay; the jungle and desert encroach; law, art, learning, religion and morality cannot be maintained like buildings, but have to be written on the hearts of each new generation. Threats to such values come more from criticism and revolution than from natural forces. Culture is, finally, plural and diverse – all societies are always involved in laborious efforts to hold together in tolerable conflict the efforts of diverse people and groups to achieve and conserve many goods. Such cultures 'are forever seeking to combine peace with prosperity, justice with order, freedom with welfare, truth with beauty, scientific truth with moral good, technical proficiency with practical wisdom, holiness with life, and all these with the rest'.[4]

One highly influential application of these more general observations is the management guru Peter Drucker's much-quoted but nowhere-recorded remark, 'Culture eats strategy for breakfast.' The insight doesn't seek to denigrate strategy, but to contrast a generic, imposed method with an authentic, unique and owned culture, and to recognize that if your organization's culture doesn't align with the leadership's strategy, the culture will always win. It has become a mantra for management consultants and organizational theorists the world over. Among the insights derived from this mantra are claims like, 'people are loyal to culture, not to strategy', 'culture is more efficient than strategy', 'advertising is a tax you pay for having an unremarkable culture', and 'culture provides greater discipline than disciplinary action does'.[5] Such insights appeal to management experts because they suggest that while a company's bottom line for the coming year will be determined by strategy, its bottom line for subsequent years will be determined by culture. In other words, a culture plan is, in the long term, more important than a strategic plan. This vividly demonstrates that culture isn't a static, given phenomenon best seen by an external observer, but a dynamic, intentional power shaped by the close attention of participants and reflecting their most profound but often unspoken commitments.

Culture in particular

While Niebuhr perceives the all-pervasive quality of culture as the way human beings shape and adapt to nature, and Drucker and his followers seek to enhance organizations by paying particular attention to the priority of culture over more generic strategy, culture has a second, more particular meaning, sometimes rendered in the term 'high culture'.

This notion of culture understands it as a largely separate reality from culture-in-general, representing the best and most aspirational aspects of human creation, notably fine art, performance art, and literature. Such an understanding is invariably controversial, because its quality lies in the eye of the beholder and thus seems subjective, and because its production and enjoyment tend to be restricted to a segment of the population and is thus often regarded as elitist. Nonetheless, such an understanding has its ardent proponents. In his *Culture and the Death of God*, Terry Eagleton describes how this perspective sits in the light of two significant developments: the sceptical scrutiny of postmodernism and the decline of Christendom. Eagleton offers a sustained argument about the definition, influence and extent of culture, and its role as a substitute for religion in the modern era.[6]

The story, as Eagleton lucidly tells it, goes like this. The Enlightenment sought 'to oust a barbarous, benighted faith in favour of a rational, civilised one'.[7] It tore into religion, but it did so as a child berates a parent: it resented the power of the church, particularly in the political sphere, but it never imagined being without religion, and it had few ideas about how society was to be conceived or controlled if religion were truly to leave the scene. Eagleton ridicules the confusion of those who couldn't live with religion but couldn't live without it: ' "I don't happen to believe myself, but it is politically expedient that you should" is the catchphrase of thinkers supposedly devoted to the integrity of the intellect,' he caustically observes.[8] Meanwhile, the more rigorously rational the world becomes, the more arbitrary and unfathomable God becomes. At the same time, everything in society becomes explicable, but there is no longer any system of making actions legitimate or valid. Such pathos continues into the industrial era. Individualism is a divisive doctrine, inhospitable to corporate identity; capitalism proves incapable of generating an organic ideology of its own and so reverts to one imported from else-where – often an idealized bygone era. It requires values such as faith, truth, authority and hierarchical order, but has no way of manufacturing them.

And so to the defining project of the centuries since the Enlightenment: filling God's large shoes with reason, art, culture, imagination, the nation, humanity, the state, the People, society, morality 'or some other such specious surrogate'.[9] God is not quite dead – mortally sick, perhaps, but capably delegating responsibility 'to one envoy or another, part of whose task is to convince men and women that there is no cause for alarm, that business will be conducted as usual despite the absence of the proprietor, and that the acting director is perfectly capable of handling all inquiries'.[10] The anti-climax to this narrative is postmodernism. Postmodernism is 'too young to recall a time when there was (so it is alleged) truth, unity, totality, objectivity, universals, absolute values, stable identities and rock-solid foundations, and thus finds nothing disquieting in their apparent absence'.[11] It experiences 'no fragmentation, since unity was an illusion all along; no false consciousness, because no unequivocal truth; no shaking of the foundations, since none to be dislodged'. Truth and identity have not vanished; they never were. For modernism, the death of God is a trauma – a source of anguish as well as celebration. By contrast, postmodernism doesn't experience it at all. There is nothing missing – no tragedy. 'The postmodern subject is hard-pressed to find enough depth and continuity in itself to be a suitable candidate for tragic self-dispossession. You cannot give away a self you never had.'[12] There is nowhere for God to dwell – no starry heaven above and no interior castle within.

Eagleton accepts the twofold understanding of culture I have described above. On the one hand, as in Niebuhr's understanding, culture is a descriptive, anthropological category, describing value, language, symbol, kinship, heritage and community in social habit and interaction; on the other hand, culture is a normative, aesthetic term, associated with the tastes of an elite, notably found in the hope that art will prove to be humanity's salvation. Eagleton's central point is that religion was the force that united and harmonized these two senses of culture. Nothing else could – which is why being an atheist was harder than it appeared. Eagleton tells how in the nineteenth century 'myth, art and culture (and the greatest of these is culture) sought to become ersatz forms of religion. They were the means by which transcendent truths might be converted into the currency of common experience.'[13] Hovering in the background of this narrative – named, but never explored – is the most perverse alternative: nationalism. Eagleton identifies the issue thus:

> For a certain vein of Romantic nationalism, the nation, like the Almighty himself, is sacred, autonomous, indivisible, without end or origin, the ground of being, the source of identity, the principle of human unity, a champion of the dispossessed and a cause worth dying for.

Eagleton points out, tantalizingly, how the prime current candidate for religion is sport – with its liturgical assemblies, sacred icons, revered traditions and pantheon of heroes.[14] Sport is also culture – understood as both common habit and elite artistry. This is how Eagleton assesses the contemporary scene, at least in the West:

> As the power of religion begins to fail, its various functions are redistributed like a precious legacy to those seeking to become its heirs. Scientific rationalism takes over its doctrinal certainties, while radical politics inherits its mission to transform the face of the earth. Culture in the aesthetic sense safeguards something of its spiritual depth. Indeed, most aesthetic ideas (creation, inspiration, unity, autonomy, symbol, epiphany and so on) are really displaced fragments of theology. Signs which accomplish what they signify are known as poetry to aesthetics and as sacraments to theology.[15]

Eagleton summarizes the similarity between art and religion by pointing out that both used to be matters of great public contention, but have withdrawn into the seclusion of private expression.

> Religion follows the trajectory of art and sexuality, those other two major constituents of what one might call the symbolic sphere. They, too, tend to pass out of public ownership into private hands as the modern age unfolds. The art which once praised God, flattered a patron, entertained a monarch or celebrated the military exploits of the tribe is now for the most part a question of individual self-expression. Even if it is not confined to a garret, it does not typically conduct its business amidst the bustle of court, church, palace or public square. At the same time, Protestantism finds God in the inmost recesses of the individual life. It is when artists, like bishops, are unlikely to be hanged that we can be sure that modernity has set in. They do not matter enough for that.[16]

H. Richard Niebuhr and Terry Eagleton give us the shape of our challenge. Faith and art need to accept that they are part of culture in a general sense. But they must not accept that they dwell simply in the private sphere of taste and expression. At a time when understandings of the human are shrinking, yet are more needed than ever, art and religion have opportunities that they can take together in ways that they may not be able to access apart.[17]

Two proposals for a renewal of faith and culture

I want to look at two contemporary proposals for a renewal of faith and culture. The first comes from artist and theologian Makoto Fujimura. Fujimura advocates for a spirit of generosity that awaits genesis moments that have generative capacity. He laments what he regards as the two pollutants in the river of culture: over-commodification of art and utilitarian pragmatism. He describes how artists, horrified by the Holocaust and nuclear warfare, came to see themselves as secular prophets and priests with a call to speak the truth against the Establishment. They isolated themselves from mainstream society and sought to shock people into perceiving the scandals of their era, producing an artistic *via negativa*, emphasizing what truth is not. But their work became more esoteric and elitist. Then art became conscripted into the culture wars as a frontline foot soldier defending freedom of expression against tradition and conformity. Much was swept away and most of what was left was commercialism, where creativity is given over to survival and the celebrity model of art prevails.

Fujimura's diagnosis is bleak:

> Today an artist cannot simply paint; a novelist cannot simply write; a pianist cannot simply play. Utilitarian pragmatism and commercialism so thoroughly pervade culture that without some shift in worldview and expectation, what we do as artists – the activities of the arts – will be neither sustainable nor generative.[18]

Reacting to the culture wars, and the way they have weaponized the arts, particularly in the United States, Fujimura asserts, 'Culture is not a territory to be won or lost but a resource we are called to steward with care. Culture is a garden to be cultivated.'[19] Recalling how T. S. Eliot, in his *Notes towards the Definition of Culture*, maintained that culture may be described as 'that which makes life worth living',[20] Fujimora calls on artists and their friends to see this as a genesis moment in which they can find a truly prophetic voice, 'acting not just for shock and self-aggrandizement but for cultivation and common flourishing. Artists can become known instead as "citizen artists" who lead in society with their imagination and their work.'[21]

Following Lewis Hyde and Wendell Berry, Fujimura perceives that art exists in two economies, the market and the gift economy – but that the latter is fundamental. He recalls how Native Americans in the Pacific Northwest regarded salmon as a gift, taking no more than was necessary and trusting stocks would replenish. When settlers came, salmon turned into a commodity, and in no time market forces jeopardized its survival. Art is like that salmon: in just the same way, it needs some protection from market forces to survive. Fujimura maintains, 'It's not enough to have artists who seek after beauty, truth and goodness; we must have churches, policies and communities that promote a long-term nurture of culture that is beautiful, truthful, and full of goodness.'[22] He prefers the metaphor of garden to greenhouse, since the latter are sheltered, resource-intensive and less vibrant; a garden has a better balance of wind and rain, yet within an enclosed space.

Hence Fujimura arrives at the image of an estuary, where salt water mixes with fresh, in a confluence of river and tidal waters. An estuary is an environment not of protection but of preparation. Estuaries

> are a critical nursery area, for example, for young salmon, striped bass, and other fish that come downstream after hatching. Life in semi-protected estuarial wetlands during a critical period in their development readies these fish for life in the ocean . . . [Estuaries'] purpose is not so much *protection* as *preparation*. Each individual habitat strengthens its participants to interact with the wider environment, making for a diversity that is healthy enough for true competition.[23]

Fujimura sees artists as oysters, cleaning the water they inhabit, often turning pollutants into pearls, yet sometimes purifying the water at the cost of polluting themselves. Oysters are found in estuaries. He cites significant 'estuary' periods in history, such as sixteenth-century Japan, with the influx of Portuguese and Italian missionaries, early twentieth-century New York, with many immigrants and influences from the American South, pre-Renaissance Europe, where Ottoman invasions brought Islamic and Asian stimuli, and the salons of eighteenth- and nineteenth-century Paris. Such estuaries come about today when three elements converge: the creative capital of an artist, the social capital of a pastor or community leader, and the material capital of finance or business. Fujimura maintains that a movement requires two of these to be sustainable, but all three to flourish; the difference is that while material capital is limited, creative and social capital are infinite. Creating cultural estuaries in churches, schools and informal associations is his strategy for enhancing culture.

A second proposal for the renewal of faith and culture comes from Rowan Williams. In his book *Grace and Necessity: Reflections on Art and Love*, Williams provides a counterbalance to Makoto Fujimura.[24] Drawing on the work of the mid-twentieth-century French Roman Catholic philosopher Jacques Maritain, Williams is careful to avoid a too-hasty connection between art and morality, either as grounds or purpose. Maritain follows Thomas Aquinas and Aristotle in distinguishing between making and doing. Doing is the right use of freedom for the sake of human good; making is the production of a specific outcome in the material world – a product. To make well is not the same as to do well: 'virtuous making aims not at the good of humanity but at the good of what is made.'[25] Maritain adopts Thomas Aquinas' definition of beauty as 'that which pleases when seen'. He goes on to say:

> A feature may be in itself jarring or even terrible, but may still be 'what pleases' in its context. Beauty is not, therefore, a single transcendent object or source of truth – that is it provides satisfaction, joy, for the human subject, but it does not in itself *tell* you anything.

Thus there are three levels in the life of a finished work: first, integrity, the inner logic of a product; next, proportion, its harmony and adaptation to the observer's mind; then what Maritain calls splendour – the active drawing-in of the observer's mind.[26]

Thus beauty

is a relation between work and observer in which the observer's will as well as intellect is engaged, a relation in which what is present to the mind is sensed as desirable, as a source of pleasure. But what Maritain is, I think, cautioning against is any suggestion that the sensation of being in the presence of the desirable gives you any information about how the world actually is or about what is humanly to be done about it. Given that the human will is spectacularly fallible and self-deceiving, a judgement of beauty cannot as such be morally or metaphysically illuminating.[27]

Williams adds that 'when we apprehend that something is not there solely for me, that it has an overplus of significance, this very fact has a metaphysical dimension'.[28] The gratuitous, disinterested character of the artefact means that awareness of beauty is a recognition of something beyond the merely functional in a work. But crucially, 'the production of beauty cannot be a goal for the artist.'[29] If the artist sets out to please, it will compromise the end product. Nonetheless, if it is well and honestly made it will exhibit that overflow of presence that generates joy. Yet Maritain accepts that beauty is always incomplete – limping, like Jacob after tussling with the angel: he speaks of 'that kind of imperfection through which infinity wounds the finite'.[30]

Towards a vision for church and the arts

It's time to review what we have learned from the two senses of culture and the two proposals and suggest a theological vision for the arts. Here are four proposals.

First, the church is a work of art. God is the artist, who makes the church, through the action of the Holy Spirit, in the form of Christ, out of the material of human beings. As Williams points out, finitude means that all works of art are incomplete; the church without question evidences 'that kind of imperfection through which infinity wounds the finite'. The church is not beautiful, in a detached, distant sense: but if and when it is well and honestly made, it exhibits that overflow of presence that generates joy. The church has exactly that over-plus or surfeit of significance to which Williams alludes. It has that beauty derived from a recognition of something beyond the merely functional in its life and flourishing. And yet those who seek to build up the church, those who bless the church without being desirous or feeling worthy to be its members, and the Holy Spirit who draws diverse people into its life, are all seeking something other than beauty – more likely the word of truth or the gesture of goodness – rather than beauty itself. No one is setting out to look fine or noble or elegant; but in aiming to be true and striving to be good their labours can sometimes, perhaps most often in retrospect, and often in the context of failure, be appropriately described as beautiful. The words of Ephesians 2.10, translated blandly in the NRSV as 'we are what [God] has made us', sometimes 'God's work-manship', could more imaginatively be rendered 'we are God's work of art', or perhaps better, 'God's poem'. It's against the grain of the New Testament to assume that 'we' means an assortment of individuals: 'we' means the church, and the whole of Ephesians 2.1–10 is about the lengths to which God has gone to make the church a companion for ever.

Thus the church isn't initially a community that does or makes things, or even an environment that enables and encour-ages things to be done and made; it's fundamentally a thing that has been made, an artefact, the fruit of Christ's labours and the constant activity of the Holy Spirit. As Christ made the Forth Rail Bridge by laying down his life, so the Holy Spirit contin-ues daily to paint and maintain it so that the world can cross it; but the wonder of crossing it and the spectacle of beholding it means that a structure built for a specific purpose is now regarded just as much as a thing of beauty. What this means for the church is that art isn't an instrumental thing – 'a good way of getting the message across in a visual age' – but a cel-ebration and imitation of the way the church is itself a work of art. Thus art is a sacrament – a tangible item or practice that honours, echoes and replicates a truth embodied in the life, death and resurrection of Christ. Art isn't always simply beautiful, just as not all actions of Christ are simply beautiful; but art in myriad ways recalls and reproduces the prophetic, priestly and kingly ministries of Jesus.[31]

Second, following Eagleton, the church can once again be a place that unites and harmonizes the two senses of culture – the anthropological and the aesthetic, culture as social habit and interaction, and culture as creation, inspiration and epiphany. The church long ago gave up the claim to be *the* place of unity and harmony; such an accolade is not its own to bestow: but it can nonetheless seek to be *a* place, indeed, an exemplary such place. Church means, in popular speech, almost equally a sacred space where people gather to pray and find sanctuary, and at the same time the people who gather there, an institution with visible leaders, active participants and fringe adherents. It is thus a place and a people. The place is one in which art can be displayed, song can be sung, dance and drama performed; the people are ones who, collectively and individually, host, encourage and respond to these arts, and offer fertile soil in which artistic culture interacts with social culture. But in Eagleton's sense, as a meeting point of the anthropological and the aesthetic, church may also have a third meaning – as a verb, or at least an adverb, a how and not just a what, a way of configuring dialogue and fomenting debate, of fostering awe and inviting response, of seeing patiently and listening carefully, of tempering instant reaction and cultivating generous reception.

If the first assertion was that the church was God's work of art, this second assertion is that the church is like a parable. A parable is an image, story or parody, a mirror or a challenge, which follows the logic of God and discloses the outcomes of that logic in startling and vivid ways. A parable portrays the surprise, reversal, delight, consternation and revelation of God's grace and mercy, judgement and truth. Along the way it has a variety of characters who take up roles in representing God's ways. A parable is not a fable with a moral, after the manner of Aesop; neither is it a device for communicating a proposition that could be succinctly expressed in other ways. It is an invitation to enter God's upside-down kingdom, and perceive the action and character of God in the midst of human fragility, fear and folly. The church is precisely that: the living-out of an alternative story, the logical outworking of a rival truth, the daily and weekly rehearsing of a different method, results and conclusion. It is not just a work of art, but a gallery of alternative lives, intriguing plots, compelling suggestions.

If the church is a public parable, singing a different song, it cannot content itself with the role of commentator or peripheral observer. It's not enough to call on government to do more, corporations to be more righteous, celebrities to be better role models, institutions to live more honourably. It's not prophetic to call others continually to change. The church must exhibit the change it wants others to make. It must be a living alternative. It must embody the generosity it seeks, offer the wisdom it demands, celebrate the new order it proclaims. It must *be* a parable, not just tell one.

Third, Fujimura's image of an estuary offers a humble but intriguing reassessment of what the church thinks it's doing. One might say the church has long assumed it was the sea, to which every river led. Or it might be said to have identified with the pure water of the river, in contrast with the salty water of the sea. But the image of an estuary is helpful for a church regarding itself as a meeting place of human and divine, gospel and culture, timeless truth and embodied experience, word and world. Church means the Spirit-empowered intersection of human and divine, incarnate in Jesus, now continuing beyond his ascension; it means local communities of disciples, worshipping, sharing, growing, walking in faith and hope; and it means those institutional structures that facilitate both of the above. But it also, in the great majority of cases, means a building; and very often that building has a significance in a neighbourhood (sometimes beyond that neighbourhood) that exceeds its purpose as a gathering-place for the faithful. For this reason the metaphor of a transitional place where cross-fertilization can take place and creativity can thrive amid diverse conversation partners may be apt. Churches work hard to make themselves inspiring locations where people are drawn into a sense of the presence of God; but they can work equally hard to make themselves hospitable locations where people of varied backgrounds may gather in a spirit of mutual appreciation, generous regard and constructive challenge. The two purposes of church need not be mutually exclusive.

Art is a perfect example of how such an estuary space may flourish. A congregation may encourage art on three levels. One is the participatory: a local church may host an artists' and craftspeople's group; it may take participants of all abilities; there's no reason why it can't host members of all faiths and none; perhaps each month a member of the group may be invited to exhibit their work in a valued and visible place, and be given the opportunity to write or speak about it. Another is the aspirational: a competition might be held for an artefact to be placed permanently in the church building, tenders invited, donors sought, publicity encouraged, visitors attracted. Similar approaches might apply for temporary art installations. A third level is the commercial. A church building might be a suitable venue for a display and sale of artworks; yet another host of new faces drawn in, conversations triggered, relationships made; and the church perhaps takes a 20 per cent cut of all pieces sold. In a short time a secluded, secretive space may be opened out to become a centre of community activity, energy and creativity. Much the same principles and categories would apply for choral music or drama or literature. What's needed is for a church to let go of the need for direct outcomes and linear trajectories and to let the Holy Spirit govern the interactions and catalyse its own surprises.

Fourth, following Drucker and Williams, the church's unique ability should be to be a culture free from anxiety. If sin and hurt have been healed by the forgiveness of sins, and if terror and horror have been displaced by the promise of everlasting life, the church does not have to be locked into the conventional measurements of papering over its mistakes and managing its future. The culture of the church should be one that has time to be hospitable (because it's God's time), has eagerness to listen (because it's God's truth), is open to the stranger (because thus we entertain God's angels), is unafraid to embark on faithful experiments (because God determines the outcome) and is glad to play (because all it needs to do is to imitate the joy of God's kingdom). The culture that eats strategy for breakfast is the culture made possible by forgiveness and eternal life.

Thus as Williams following Maritain puts it, the production of beauty is not the church's goal. If the church sets out to please, it will compromise the end product. Yet if it lives well and honestly it will indeed exhibit that overflow of presence that generates joy. The church models art by allowing its beauty to be ancillary. It is seeking something even deeper and richer than beauty – but if it finds what it is looking for, it will be able to look back and see that its route there was beautiful. The church's engagement in culture is not to instrumentalize culture in order to communicate a detachable message, nor to suppose culture can replace religion as the sum of human aspiration, nor yet to assume that all truth lies within ourselves and enabling it to be expressed is the only way to let that truth speak. It is to become, through the possibilities, imagination and relationships art makes possible, a culture that evinces infectious generosity and irrepressible creativity, exciting and inspiring people to perceive and embody the kingdom of God. When a management guru says 'advertising is a tax you pay for having an unremarkable culture', the hope is that such a marketing expert would look at a church that had truly embraced the possibility of culture and say, 'See – that's exactly what I mean.' In the end, if church is adverb not noun, it does not have a culture – it *is* a culture.

The vision in action

In conclusion, I want to describe how this fourfold vision – of artwork, parable, estuary and culture – might take shape. Because of the perpetual concern of elitism I am going to tell a story from a humble place, yet a place where all four of these dimensions were significant.

For the six years either side of the millennium I was vicar of a parish in Norwich. Norwich is known for its ancient city centre with its countless medieval churches. But this parish was a 1930s council estate three miles to the west. Six years before I arrived, the diocese had built a very modern church to replace the dilapidated hall that previously housed Christian worship at the heart of the estate. From the outset the new building suffered relentless vandalism. Once I was asked by a teenage girl, 'Are you the new vicar?' I said, 'I've been here about three years.' 'I used to know the old vicar,' she replied. 'I used to throw stones at his windows.' 'Why was that?' I asked, genuinely interested. 'Oh, you see,' she said, matter-of-factly, 'I don't believe in God.'

In fact, the stone-throwing wasn't limited to the building, but sometimes extended to the congregation as they left worship. There were times in my first year or two when the evening service felt like a siege. The 20 ground-floor windows were replaced by protected Perspex, and a daunting iron gate prevented people gathering to drink in the open porch.

The congregation and I got busy. We hosted countless community activities, often at little or no rent. We opened up the church to a youth club, for up to 50 young people at a time. We invited schoolchildren to make huge 30-foot-long paper murals to put on the walls, representing the different seasons of the church year. We gave cameras to single mothers to photograph local characters and display their pictures and words around the sanctuary. We had a huge dance troupe that rehearsed and performed constantly. We joined local committees and trustees, seeking to improve the neighbourhood together. We ran after-school and holiday clubs until we were worn out.

The name of the church was St Elizabeth's. Quickly I came to identify with this figure from Luke's Gospel like never before. Elizabeth was old. As Genesis says of Sarah, 'it had ceased to be with her after the manner of women.' Nothing more was expected of her life. Likewise the housing estate was around

65 years old and no one inside or out looked to it with any degree of expectation. Yet our daily prayer was that this church and this estate would be blessed, and become a blessing to others.

Any new minister knows that one of the things you have to do before accepting a job is to look over the church accounts, because they'll tell you a story no one will convey face to face. And so it was I discovered the existence of a fund called 'Stained Glass Windows'. It seemed the last thing in the world the church needed. It turned out it was a fund left over from the old hall, intended to make the building look more like a church. But three years after I came we did an extraordinary thing. In two 4 × 4 foot windows, only three feet from the ground, we put a stained-glass depiction of the meeting of Mary and Elizabeth. In the left window was Mary: young, overwhelmed, yet full of joy. In the right window was Elizabeth: old, forsaken, weighed down by the world, yet astonished and filled with the Holy Spirit, and exclaiming with a loud cry, 'Why has this happened to me?', at just the very moment the child in her womb leaps for joy. None of us could quite believe that in the very place where countless windows had been smashed just four or five years before, we were now inserting such glorious stained-glass windows that spoke to the apparently godforsaken nature of the estate and yet the youthfulness of many who lived there, and anticipated the blessing that God would bring to the whole community.

A year later, inspired by the success of the windows, we set about taking down the iron gates. More than anything else, those gates were a symbol of how frightened the congregation had become of those who so often expressed their antagonism in violent ways. The gates were transported to what was then called the Norwich School of Art, and a young woman, not much older than the Mary of Luke's birth narrative, began a long process of transforming these oppressive railings into an extraordinary 40-foot-wide wing – an awesome and breath-taking symbol of the Holy Spirit, which almost entirely filled the space above the entrance to the sanctuary of the church. It was the most remarkable turning of a sword into a ploughshare I've ever seen.

The effect on the congregation was as awesome as these two extraordinary works of art. The windows made us believe that, despite adversity and hostility, we really did belong in this community and we really did have a gospel that spoke to the heart of the community's story. And the wing inspired us to trust that what was going to happen would not depend on our strength, but that, waiting on the Lord, we would mount up with wings like eagles, we would run and not be weary, we would walk and not faint.

This experience for me encapsulated the paradox of the incarnation. On the one hand, it was too ordinary. Everyone knows the jokes about Norwich: the graveyard of ambition, a town in decline since the fourteenth century, whose doctors take a quick assessment of the state of mind of their presenting patients and write above the bed the letters NFN – 'Normal for Norfolk'. Here was a neighbourhood so behind the times that, 20 years after the Thatcher government's right to buy scheme, 90 per cent of the houses were still council-owned. This was a community apparently summed up by Nathanael's words in John's Gospel, 'Can anything good come out of Nazareth?' I remember walking out of the vicarage and seeing a boy kicking a football against the church, and saying, 'Can I ask why you'd want to do that? This is your church and your community. I can understand why you'd kick a ball at another church in another neighbourhood, but why destroy what belongs to you?' Just too ordinary, too flawed, too painfully human.

But here was an incarnate church, communicating in practical gestures and open heart that God cared about what people cared about. Here was this depiction of a babe in the womb leaping for joy, a whole community rising up on eagles' wings, a glimpse of the wondrous and eternal in the midst of despondency and doldrums. It was just too extraordinary. It was saying just exactly what the first chapter of Luke's Gospel is saying, which is that God does the most extraordinary things through the most ordinary people. God chooses an obscure part of the Roman province of Syria, a town of Nazareth, to begin the most extraordinary story of all. God puts an underage, unmarried girl together with an overage, exhausted woman to make the setting for an exhilarating declaration. God is turning the ordinary texture of human existence into the astonishing glory of divine essence. Jesus is at the same time totally and utterly ordinary and astoundingly and gloriously extraordinary.

In my office I keep on my bookshelf framed photographs of those two stained-glass windows, Mary and Elizabeth, as a constant reminder of how God does the extraordinary through the most ordinary. They ask me Elizabeth's perpetual and ambiguous question, 'Why has this happened to me?' One day just a few years ago I got a parcel from Norwich with a framed photograph inside. It was a third stained-glass image, which, 15 years later, had been placed in the window beside the first two. The window depicts St Anne, the apocryphal mother of Mary, grandmother of Jesus, aunt of Elizabeth, by the same artist in just the same style. I carefully placed Anne beside Mary and Elizabeth on my bookshelf. I remembered that community, all our failures and successes, most of all those projects that opened heaven to earth and lifted us up on eagles' wings. And I thought, 'God is faithful. God is still becoming extraordinarily divine in ordinary flesh. This is what true beauty looks like. This is incarnation. Jesus is being born.'

Here we see each dimension of our vision for church and the arts. This was the church as a work of art: not a thing of beauty, but a canvas on to which the Holy Spirit was painting a previously unknown image. This was the church as a parable of crucifixion yielding resurrection. This was the church as estuary, where taking the risk of opening the building to a kaleidoscope of community events eventually led to perceiving the pearl in the oyster of the stained glass and the huge sculpture. And this, finally, was church as culture: thrilling as the two artefacts were, the key was that church and neighbourhood found a common point that exceeded the previous best efforts of either of them, and found peace and celebration in the beautiful things that became possible when they were able to work together. That is what opening a church's soul to possibilities of culture can do.

Notes

1 H. R. Niebuhr, *Christ and Culture* (New York: Harper and Row, 1951), pp. 29–39 at 32.

2 Niebuhr, *Christ and Culture*, p. 256.

3 Niebuhr, pp. 36–7.

4 Niebuhr, pp. 38–9.

5 See for example Joe Tye, '12 Reasons Culture Eats Strategy for Lunch', www.slideshare.net/joetye/12-reasons-culture-eats-strategy-for-lunch-25988674/73-The_Cultural_Blueprinting_Toolkit_features.

6 Terry Eagleton, *Culture and the Death of God* (New Haven and London: Yale University Press, 2014).

7 Eagleton, p. 12.

8 Eagleton, p. 207.

9 Eagleton, p. 151.

10 Eagleton, p. 151.

11 Eagleton, p. 185.

12 Eagleton, p. 186.

13 Eagleton, p. 80.

14 Eagleton, p. 45.

15 Eagleton, p. 174.

16 Eagleton, p. 2.

17 Raymond Williams notes that the word culture, which he describes as 'one of the two or three most complicated words in the English language . . . because it has now come to be used for important concepts in several distinct intellectual disciplines and in several distinct and incompatible systems of thought', originally referred to husbandry. This basic connection to cultivation and the soil he sees as a counterweight to the tendency to associate the term with high culture. Raymond Williams, *Keywords*, rev. edn (New York: Oxford University Press, 1983), pp. 87–93.

18 Makoto Fujimura, *Culture Care: Reconnecting with Beauty for our Common Life* (Downers Grove: IVP, 2017), p. 38.

19 Fujimura, p. 40.

20 T. S. Eliot, *Notes Towards the Definition of Culture* (New York: Harcourt, Brace and Company, 1949), p. 26.

21 Fujimura, *Culture Care*, pp. 41–2.

22 Fujimura, p. 100.

23 Fujimura, pp. 102–4 (italics original).

24 Rowan Williams, *Grace and Necessity: Reflections on Art and Love* (London: Morehouse, 2005).

25 Williams, p. 11.

26 Williams, p. 12.

27 Williams, pp. 12–13.

28 Williams, p. 13.

29 Williams, p. 13.

30 Williams, p. 21.

31 I have written further about prophetic, priestly and kingly art in Samuel Wells, *Learning to Dream Again: Rediscovering the Heart of God* (Grand Rapids: Eerdmans, 2013), pp. 72–8. UK edition, with substantial alterations, Norwich: Canterbury Press, 2013, pp. 61–7.

6

Realizing God's Presence: On Earth as it is in Heaven

The simple thesis of this book is that engaging in commercial, compassionate and cultural initiatives, far from draining the church of energy, identity or focus, may on the contrary restore to congregations the sources of their own renewal. In the first chapter I established the economic, political and social context of this argument, and in the second chapter I identified how money represents a key indicator of how the church understands its mission. In the next three chapters I looked at how commerce, compassion and culture respectively stand to be agents of renewal. In this final chapter I return to the seven characteristics of kingdom churches to describe in more detail what a kingdom congregation looks like. In each case I seek to draw out the theological significance of the characteristic, identify what makes it distinctive, and explain what it looks like in the life of a congregation.

A community of hope

A *community* is a society or neighbourhood in which people experience a particular quality of being together and belonging. This can come about through the maintenance of long-term relationships, but also through a sense of people being accepted, understood or welcomed as who they are in a way that evokes a feeling of trust, honesty and greater self-worth. The Christmas story, for example, is all about community.

There is the new community across gender: a man and a woman find they are having a baby of whom the man is not the father, and yet they each make a step in faith to discover a truth that's beyond either of them. There's a new community across class: the shepherds, far from being excluded and despised, find first place at the manger. There's a new community across race: the Gentile Magi, distant from the customs and purity of the children of Israel, perceive a destiny for the baby king beyond what anyone in Israel can envisage. And most of all there's a new community between God and creation, a new divine–human possibility, in the face of this fully human, fully divine child – a new reality better known as communion. Community is always a window into communion; and communion – the combination of with (com) and in (union) – is the goal of all inter-human and human–divine relationship.

Meanwhile *hope* is a settled disposition to anticipate that God will act in the future either to transform and fulfil the circumstances of the present by disclosing their true purpose and end, or at least to reveal in these same events a deeper truth of relationship and destiny than is currently recognizable. The answer to 'Why is this happening to me?' is not simply 'There is no reason' or 'Everyone has their own cross to bear', however appropriate the pastoral significance of such phrases may be; it is finally either 'You will one day discover', or 'Because God is preparing to show you a truer face than you have ever seen before, and you may look back on this experience as the defining moment of your life.' Hope looks to the future not as the bringer of death, the thief of meaning or the harbinger of danger, but as the promise of revelation: the fundamental theological statement about the future is that now we see in a glass darkly, but then we shall fully know, as we are fully known.

Both community and hope are countercultural words. The significance of community is brought out by Paul's image of the body. In 1 Corinthians 12, Paul says that each part of the church, each member of the church, is like an eye or an ear or a hand. The foot can't say to the hand, 'I don't need you', nor can the eye say to the rest, 'I'm the whole body.' And Paul underlines that the weaker members of the body are vital to the health and welfare of the body.

This sense of community is vividly portrayed in Richard Adams' novel *Watership Down*. *Watership Down* is a novel about a dozen rabbits that search for a warren to call home.[1] Each of the communities the rabbits encounter has its own political system. The warren at the beginning of the novel is a traditional, hierarchical society. The rabbits run away from that warren because they correctly anticipate it's about to be destroyed by humans. The second warren the rabbits meet is run on a totalitarian model: there is one general who keeps all the other rabbits in a state of fear under a military regime. A third community of rabbits resembles a modern decadent society. The rabbits there are somewhat inebriated: food is plentiful and the living is easy. But the rabbits have lost the ability to find their own food and, more seriously, to tell the truth. They can't bring themselves to acknowledge that they're under the spell of a farmer who feeds them but also snares and kills them one by one. The fourth warren is the one the rabbits found for themselves on Watership Down.

The rabbits discover a great many things through their travels and adventures. The most important thing they discover is that they need each other. One of the rabbits is big and strong, another is quick-thinking and imaginative, a third is speedy, a fourth is fiercely loyal, a fifth is a good storyteller. The key rabbit is the smallest and clumsiest, who yet has a sixth sense that anticipates danger – like the destruction of the original warren. What makes this group of rabbits so significant is that they find ways of using the gifts of every member of the party so that they are never short of wisdom and intelligence about what comes next, or courage and strength to do what is needed. Thus the group of rabbits lives and moves and thinks as one body, rather than as a dozen separate bodies. There can't be such a thing as an idea or a development that is good for one of the rabbits yet not good for the whole body.

To be a part of a group like those rabbits is an experience of what community can be. One of the reasons schools and universities encourage team sports is to give their pupils and students the opportunity to join a group that will only succeed if it has a mixture of speed, size, strength, hand–eye coordination, determination, courage and imagination. The breakthrough comes when the members of the team realize it's not about any one of them being the star but about each of them discovering how much they need each other. The same is true for actors putting on a play, musicians playing in an orchestra, and singers joining a choir. The soprano doesn't say to the alto half way through *Messiah*, 'I have no need of you.'

Being one body doesn't just mean that the eye can't say to the hand, 'I have no need of you.' It means that if the eye is in pain, the whole body is in pain, and the hand does whatever it can to make things better. Paul's picture of community isn't about bland tolerance. It's about shared direction, shared wisdom and shared pain. Being one body is generally a lot more painful than going our separate ways. We spend a lot of our time searching around for vital things we have to do that make listening to one another's stories seem like a waste of time. But Paul says to us, 'Your mission is to be one body. Your message is that Christ has made you one body. There isn't anything more important for you to rush off to.'

It is when the disciples in the Acts of the Apostles become such a community that remarkable things begin to happen. But what's distinctive about the community in Acts is that it's a community of *hope* – that is to say, it's a community that looks not simply to itself to resolve its challenges but together looks to the action and revelation of God. 'God will provide' is the most provocative and astonishing utterance at the moment Abraham seems set to sacrifice his son Isaac, and 'God will provide' remains a provocative and astonishing claim today. While every politician's promise is to offer financial, material and national security, a community of hope believes such security can be found in God alone. Hope is not a wilful, taunting, reckless demand that God make an arbitrary alteration in the course of events. It is a faithful, patient expectation that God will, over time, make present the relations and conditions of the kingdom to those who in word and action anticipate its coming. Community generates hope, because those committed to one another generate momentum and expectation of what God has in store; and hope generates community, since there is nothing more infectious than seeing beautiful things happen over and over again.

In one congregation a priest began to pray in the church in silent expectation for an hour twice a week. Gradually he began to invite others to join him. Over time, the group began to make other commitments, adding study, service and sacrament to their sense of community. After a year, a formal community was formed, again adding sharing, Sabbath and stability to make a sevenfold commitment – but still with regular silent prayer of expectation at the heart of the community's life. Within six months the group had grown to 58 people, from many walks of life: some were destitute overseas nationals with no recourse to public funds, others were well-established professional people, others again had challenges with physical disability or mental ill health. The community catalysed the hope, and the hope galvanized the community. The congregation was growing not through evangelistic techniques or triumphant spiritual experiences but by the regular blessings of the God who meets people in silent prayer.

Renewed from the edge

One fundamental conviction of hope is that God gives a congregation everything it needs for a life of faithful discipleship, ministry and mission. The reason congregations frequently experience their life as scarcity is often because they are looking for resources in the wrong place. 'Can anything good come out of Nazareth?' asked Nathanael, and thereby disclosed the widespread problem that God's people were looking in the wrong place for the Messiah. Likewise the Magi search for the baby in the wrong town, the Syrian general Naaman is mystified by the unassuming nature of the prophet Elisha, and the prophets of Baal expect far more drama from the prophet Elijah. The church rapidly resorts to lament that the Spirit has abandoned it when in reality its own prejudices, habits or laziness disincline it to look towards where the Spirit is really acting.

Again, the story of *Watership Down* offers helpful examples. The rabbits illustrate the folly of ever believing it's possible to arrive – to be able to say, 'We've made it.' There is no such point of completion. Teenagers long to leave home, undergraduates long to get a degree, graduates long for a PhD or their first professional pay cheque, parents long for their first child, homeowners long to pay off the mortgage, pension-savers long for a healthy retirement. Congregations are the same. They long to clear their debts, start the mission project, finally get a minister who's a decent preacher, and sort out the music. But the moment never comes. The story of the rabbits shows us why it shouldn't: because when the dozen refugees meet the easy-living rabbits who live the good life they quite quickly see that those inebriated rabbits have lost what it takes to be a community, to tell the truth and ultimately to survive.

The church will always remain a pilgrim people. Whenever you meet a bunch of Christians who feel they've 'made it', whether in strength of numbers, firmness of doctrine, righteousness of attitude or purity of life, you can anticipate that pretty soon they'll be in trouble. Israel was formed on the way from Egypt to the Promised Land. The disciples were formed on the way from Galilee to Jerusalem. The church becomes one body as it is bound together on its common journey. It's always a work in progress.

Seeing ourselves as a pilgrim people should help us avoid the twin temptations of identifying too strongly with our culture or sealing ourselves off from it. We can't live in this culture as if it were our permanent home. But the fact we have promises to keep elsewhere doesn't make this culture inherently bad. On the contrary, the gifts God gives for the journey don't just come from one another: they often come from strangers. The rabbits in *Watership Down* receive vital help and intervention from a bird that can see things they can't, and from a young girl at a farm who saves one of the rabbits from her cat. The pilgrim church likewise must be open to receiving surprising gifts from those it might regard as strangers, like the bird, or even, like the farm girl, enemies.

The diversity of the church is a strength, not a weakness. The group of rabbits in *Watership Down* only survives because it has rabbits with different gifts, different strengths, different visions for what they are doing and where they are going. Paul says there are varieties of gifts, but the same Spirit, varieties of ways of serving God, but the same Lord. Paul may have seen it that way, but it's hardly a fashionable view among Christians today. The Bible is made up of 66 books. Each is different – some are very different from one another, and one or two even seem to contradict one another. And yet almost all Christians regard the whole Bible as God's gift to the church and as a full disclosure of God's character and purpose. The way these 66 books work together to reveal God may be an encouragement to see other denominations also as places where God is made known, and to see the diversity of Christians as a key to shaping community. If we can't do without any of the 66 books and still have all we need to know about God, how can we do without any of these other ways of being Christian? We need each other. We need each other to know God and to survive and thrive as a community. Like the eye and the hand, we cannot say to one another, 'I have no need of you.' Telling another Christian, 'I have no need of you' is really telling Jesus, 'I have no need of you.'

As I have suggested earlier, I am sceptical of the term 'inclusive' for several reasons, some practical, others theoretical. The practical reasons are that, while commendably designed to indicate an embrace of all God's children, especially those whose identities and gifts church and society have historically tended to neglect, reject or vilify, the term 'inclusive' can become simply another label – just another way of including some and excluding others, on the grounds of their not having the right or fashionable views about certain issues. Thus an inclusive church can become as narrow and selective as those congregations it seeks to challenge. Meanwhile, the epithet 'inclusive' can come to bear more weight than the noun 'church', such that the noun 'church' can cease to have much determinative resonance. Inclusion can become the only virtue, to the detriment of patience, courage, temperance, self-control or the willingness genuinely to understand why a person may be so attached to a contrary view. Being one body isn't just a matter of ignoring differences, allowing tolerance to break out, and dimming the lights to a point where all the rabbits are grey. What saves the rabbits of *Watership Down* is their willingness and commitment, at crucial moments in the narrative, to listen to one another, to hear each other out when they have stories or worries or misgivings or hopes. Out of these curious memories and visions come the gifts that make the group of rabbits so resilient and so adaptable. Being part of one body means taking the time to listen to one another's stories, stories of why one group felt it needed to break away and how another group came to be pushed out, stories of how one group came to regard as central an issue most others regard as peripheral, of how so many have felt that unity and truth were separable and that they could somehow make it on their own.

This then discloses the theoretical issue, which is that the flourishing of a genuine community of diverse views as well as identities cannot be shrunk to concentration on one aspect, that is to say, the openness of welcome. Church is of course about welcome, but welcome implies a static dichotomy of acceptance or rejection, in which attention focuses on having an enlightened attitude as regards who should be accepted. What gets lost is the notion that the church has a job to do. It's the need for hands to get busy on that job – for labourers for the harvest, as Jesus in one place puts it – that constitutes the church's appetite for diversity and open-handed welcome. Like the rabbits in *Watership Down*, the church needs all kinds of people to survive and thrive. The question that should take priority is not, 'Does your face and your lifestyle fit the criteria for being like everyone else here?' The question instead is, 'Is your heart ready and willing to accept the challenge, cost and opportunity to be commissioned to share in this task? 'Can you say the prayer of Ignatius Loyola, "Teach me to serve thee as thou deservest, to give and not to count the cost; to fight and not to heed the wounds; to toil and not to seek for rest; to labour and not to ask for any reward except that of knowing that I do thy will"?' Becoming a congregation member should not be like a naturalization process, where you have to prove you can speak the language and name past heads of state and hum the national anthem, but more like being sent down a mine, where, if you can catch the pick and are willing to shoulder the shovel, you're on the team.

In one congregation the new pastor met individually during her first three months with around a dozen members who self-identified as LBGT+. In each case she heard a similar story: 'I'm here because I don't regard my sexuality as the most interesting thing about me or about my discipleship, ministry or mission. In other places, people have chosen to make my sexuality more important than these things. I'm here because I want my baptism to be the most interesting thing about me, and because I want to be trained in discipleship, encouraged in ministry and released for mission by a congregation that isn't especially interested in my sexuality, for good or ill.' Having previously feared she might be joining a single-issue congregation where people were only interested in themselves, she was overjoyed to find quite the opposite: an outward-looking community where people supported one another in the real challenges they were each facing.

In another congregation, a group of people with an interest in disability began to plan a new kind of event: a conference designed for and led by those with lived experience of disability. In preparing the community for an influx of people with all kinds of particular needs, the group gradually taught the congregation about what making their space truly welcoming would involve. The conference took place annually for several years, and each year a new level of understanding was reached about how the gifts and perspectives of those with disabilities enriched and challenged the community as a whole. The mood changed from 'Unfortunately we can't do this' (heard as 'You can't do this because we have other priorities') to 'Of course we are going to do this, and so these are the adjustments we all need to make, just as we all need to make adjustments all the time to ensure everyone's contribution is received.'

Meeting God in adversity

The story of the Gospels is overwhelmingly one in which people in adversity come face to face with the living God made known in Jesus Christ. The historical-social reality is that Israel, returning piecemeal after 50 years of exile in Babylon, finds itself in a state of internal exile under first the Persians, then the Greeks and now the Romans, and is displaying the full range of responses, from spineless cooperation to a quest for non-political holiness to withdrawal into secluded community to outright zealot rebellion. And in encounter after encounter, Jesus meets and transforms the reality of those whose conditions in total or in part resemble the situation of Israel as a whole. At Cana it seems the wine had run out; Jesus produces too much wine. At Capernaum the heavens, in the shape of the roof, are removed, and Jesus meets a man as paralysed as Israel is. On the other side of the sea, Jesus encounters a man named after the agent of Israel's oppression, Legion, and casts evil out of his body, just as so many longed for Roman legions to be ejected from Israel. At the Galilean lake, the disciples are struggling to make any headway in ministry to Israel, when Jesus tells them to cast a missionary net on the other side of the boat and they drag in as many fish as the number of the nations, a whole new vision of mission. By the lakeshore, Peter, crestfallen by his own betrayal, is forgiven and granted a new ministry, in the words 'Feed my sheep'.

In these moments and dozens more, we are shown that God is made known to people, and to Israel and the church, most fully at their point of greatest despair and distress, when they have exhausted their own powers. Jairus has nowhere to turn as his daughter is dying. The woman with haemorrhages has suffered for no fewer than 12 years. The centurion has no power within his own culture or nation to save his dying servant. The disciples believe the boat is sinking before Jesus says, 'Hush, do not be afraid.' There seems no food to feed a thousand people before Jesus takes loaves and fishes and leaves 12 baskets over.

But these appearances are not simply, or even primarily, about a transformation of hardship into plenty. They are more consistently and explicitly about people knowing, seeing and trusting that God is with them. Mary is in despair in the garden before Jesus calls her by name. Peter is flailing in the water, when Jesus reaches out a hand to accompany him to the boat. The two disciples are making their despondent way to Emmaus, when Jesus comes alongside them and explains the scriptures to them. The terrified Peter, James and John are reeling at the sight of the transfiguration, when Jesus comes to them touches them and tells them to get up and not to be afraid.

The message is consistent and clear. Jesus is offering transfiguration of suffering, hardship and desperation, and that sometimes issues in changed circumstances, other times in transformed perceptions. Either way, it is within these challenges, more than in times of plenty and success, that disciples most often meet God – and indeed, these moments are the definitive place in which we meet God, just as in the Old Testament the key encounter with God comes when Moses is beyond the wilderness, when God declares 'I have seen . . . I have heard . . . I know . . . and I will come.'

Likewise, redemption doesn't always come to those who feel entitled to it. In Jesus' own words,

> there were many widows in Israel in the time of Elijah, when the heaven was shut up three years and six months, and there was a severe famine over all the land; yet Elijah was sent to none of them except to a widow at Zarephath in Sidon. There were also many lepers in Israel in the time of

the prophet Elisha, and none of them was cleansed except Naaman the Syrian. (Luke 4.25–7)

Renewal isn't simply restoration of the good times, not least because those times may not have been so good for everyone, but also because in God the future is always bigger than the past. Renewal is fundamentally revelation to those amid suffering, hardship and desperation, that God is with them. Most explicitly of all in the Old Testament, when Shadrach, Meshach and Abednego are in the fiery furnace, Nebuchadnezzar sees one like a son of the gods walking with them; and in the New Testament, Jesus says to the penitent thief, 'Today you will be with me in Paradise.'

Deep in the narrative of the Old Testament is a tension between the life of herdspeople, who had no fixed abode and depended intimately on the presence of God, and agrarian people, who came to rely on their crops and on the rhythms of the seasons. When Joseph saves Jacob's family and dominates Egypt through the organization of agriculture, the book of Genesis takes an ambivalent view. It is not always the case that true salvation is to be equated with guaranteed security. And when guaranteed security has been acquired, for example by Joseph, or later by Solomon entertaining the Queen of Sheba, or later still by Esther and Mordecai having displaced Haman at Ahasuerus' side, there's no indication it lasts long.

The parable of the last judgement in Matthew 25 is often used to advocate for the so-called social gospel against conventional evangelism, or to uphold the view that faith without works is dead. But part of the power of the parable is to ask the reader, 'Where are you hungry? Where are you thirsty? Where are you naked? Where are you a stranger? Where are you sick? Where are you in prison?' and, having uncovered the places of our nakedness, the aspects we fear to be revealed when we encounter the rawness of others' distress, the parts that defeat our desire to come before the judgement seat clothed in our achievements, professionalism, possessions and polite distance, to incline our hearts to expect those to be our places of encounter with God.

A congregation longing to meet God in Christ could do well to name and audit its answers to these same questions. Where are you hungry? Where are you thirsty? Where are you naked? Where are you a stranger? Where are you sick? Where are you in prison?' This is a preparation not for boasting but for an encounter based on humble recognition of need.

One congregation had a group set aside to be trained in pastoral care, specifically visiting the recently bereaved in their homes. A few times a year the group would meet together to compare notes and offer examples of best practice, as well as to share appropriately when a particularly challenging or demanding set of circumstances had arisen. The group would reflect on the past, and assist one another in recognizing the depth of these wonderings: 'I wonder what part of your life you look back on with most thankfulness. I wonder what part of your life you look back on as the time when you felt closest to God. I wonder what part of your life you find most difficult to reflect on. I wonder at what part of your life you feel you were most fully alive.' Then the group would reflect on the present, and on these wonderings: 'I wonder whom you most want to spend time with at the moment, and why. I wonder how many people will let you be sad, without trying to distract you or cheer you up. I wonder if there is a conversation you need to have with someone now, about something that maybe happened some time ago. I wonder if there is someone whom you have not forgiven; or whom you have not thanked; or who does not know how much you love them.' Finally, the group would ponder the future, through these two wonderings: 'I wonder what is the worst thing that can happen. (And I wonder what would happen next.) I wonder what is the best thing that can happen. (And I wonder what would happen next.)'

Gradually the group realized that their experience of offering ministry, in visiting the bereaved and of receiving ministry, in the discoveries they made together in their regular meetings, coalesced. But at the same time this became the most dynamic and energized group in the whole congregation, since each member was finding truth, courage and divine encounter in what they had hitherto regarded as their most benighted places. They looked forward to their visits, and even more to their meetings, as moments to recognize the presence of God.

Inspired by enterprise

It's frequently pointed out that Paul was a tentmaker and Jesus was a carpenter. These insights have often been presented as enriching a disciple's sense of calling to be both a wage earner in the world and a faithful member of the church.

But the key is for a congregation to get past the individual desire to live a righteous life, worthy of heavenly reward, and seek a corporate goal subject to corporate evaluation and judgement. It's impossible to consider business in the context of congregational life without reflecting on the parable of the talents.

The parable works on three levels. In the first place, Jesus is the talents themselves. For, in sending Jesus, the Father didn't bury God's love for creation in a hole dug in the ground; instead, the Father took that love to market, to trade with it, to face the risks and sufferings and dangers of relationship and encounter. The five talents are the incarnation – God risking everything to be with us; the five more talents are Jesus' resurrection – the proof that we will be with God for ever.

In the second place, Jesus is the master. Jesus is not a cunning manipulator, who gives us mysterious talents and then lies in wait to see whether we fail to use them properly. Instead, Jesus is a boundlessly generous friend who goes away and gives us far more than we want or need to imitate him in his absence. If we assume he's a generous friend, we'll experience the miracle and abundance of life in the Spirit. If we take him for a cunning manipulator we'll experience life as miserable scarcity.

In the third place, the church is the slaves. This parable comes at the very end of Jesus' ministry, by which time the disciples have seen the extent of what God has been doing in Jesus. The way they use their massive gifts from Jesus, in other words the Holy Spirit, is by doing the things Jesus did, spending time with the people he spent time with, breaking bread with notorious sinners and facing the criticism of the powerful. We have been shown what standards of success Jesus lived by: so success for the disciples means success in imitating Jesus.

When the master returns, it becomes clear the talents are the ways of the kingdom Jesus has given the church. Jesus says, 'You spent a lot of time with me to learn how I do business. I gave you these gifts so you could do business the way I do business. And you have, with the same result. Well done.' But then it comes to light that the third slave, who was given all the gifts Jesus bestowed upon the church, has done nothing with them. Jesus is bewildered. 'You never realized that the Eucharist was a meal where all kinds of people could gather round my table, rich and poor, women and men, skilled and unskilled, academic stars and those with special educational needs, black, Hispanic, Chinese, Indian subcontinent, Arab, Caucasian, all of them bringing different things to the table and each receiving back the same? You never realized that baptism was the moment when all your foolishness and pride, all your evil and malice, could be washed away and you could be incorporated into the way God is redeeming the world? You never realized that reading scripture invites you into a constant discovery of God's character and a revelation of the way God has already redeemed the world? You never realized that in prayer you could open your whole heart to God and find that God's whole heart is opened up to you?' It is this wilful misreading of God's character and the witness of Jesus' ministry that brings about the third slave's moment of reckoning.

The parable of the talents is thus a challenge not so much to an individual disciple on a career choice but to a congregation as a whole on whether and how to engage in the ways of the world in the manner of the kingdom. There is no explicit prescription of what kind of activities to invest in. There is simply a confident assumption that Jesus has already offered a model of how to go about God's business in the world, and an encouragement to take the risk of making a start. The parable provides no consolation to those who wish to keep the church's nose clean by withdrawing to a place of righteous aloofness.

One helpful way of conceiving the distinction between the slaves who put the talents to use and the one who didn't is made by Greg Jones. He distinguishes between holders and handlers:

> Holders are expected to preserve the thing. 'Hold my Coke while I run into the store' means 'I want my Coke to be in its current shape when you return it.' Handlers, on the other hand, are typically expected to *engage the thing*. We misspeak when we say, 'Hold my baby while I run into the store,' because we really want that baby handled.[2]

Jones goes on to say:

> Only humble people can suspend their own will in order to pay attention to the will of another will or person, and only humble people are trusted to do something radically new with something deeply treasured. Traditionalists hold; bearers of a tradition handle. Traditionalists grasp whatever they treasure . . . They hold it so tightly that they squeeze its life out . . . Within a tradition, the treasure lies in being an active participant in its growth, with a posture of cultivation rather than preservation.[3]

Discovering talents

Management experts have begun to expose the folly that diversity is something to be *managed*. The crucial argument is that creativity increases with diversity and decreases with conformity. Just as important as race, class and gender diversity is 'an organization that can accommodate differences in perspective, habits of mind, core assumptions, and worldviews, and then go beyond accommodation to create a place where difference is celebrated and even leveraged to add value'.[4] It's possible to have a commendably diverse leadership – all urbane, sophisticated multilingual, diplomatic and mildly humorous – drawn from all over the globe, and yet find a group that doesn't rock the boat, question procedure or let its individual gifts shine.[5] By contrast, the London Organising Committee of the Olympic Games and Paralympic Games went significantly further. According to one account, its

> Trailblazer Programme was designed to ensure that people of all ages could apply to be 'early entry volunteers.' In the words of [its HR director], 'We had retired accountants, auditors from the City, school teachers, car park attendants, skilled workers – people from all walks of life alongside paid staff – both sides learned from each other.' It became, in effect, a 'learning to work with difference' initiative.
>
> . . . After a few years working with the committee . . . employees were much more likely to voluntarily declare themselves gay or lesbian in data relating to sexual orientation . . . You can see that a clever diversity and inclusion strategy takes you to difference beyond diversity.[6]

The key to the whole strategy was that diversity was regarded as an asset, not a problem. Thus does an orientation towards the creative arts and the encouragement of free expression link closely with a dynamic understanding of inclusion – not about everyone's right to be here but about the need for everyone's gifts to be harnessed if the organization is to exceed its goals and be the best it can be.

In one congregation, a dispirited group recognized they weren't sure how they could really engage with their neighbourhood, which as well as having a very varied residential community was surrounded by national cultural institutions. The congregation set about initiating a festival of arts, community and heritage, to celebrate the life of the church and the life of the neighbourhood. It quickly became an integral part of the church's year, and after very few years began to be seen as an exciting part of local life. There were sculpture exhibitions, tea parties, battle re-enactments, discussions, audience-centred concerts, an evening of new protest songs, inter-religious and intercultural celebrations, debates, and more parties, all seeking to influence the future by asking questions about issues such as urban pollution that affected the whole community. The congregation underpinned the festival through hands-on work and through financial support. This involvement helped build strong links with local organizations that now saw the church as having something to offer, and also helped the neighbourhood's sense of itself as a place distinct from the larger cluster of national cultural institutions.

Humbled by repentance

The season of Lent begins with the words, 'Dust you are, and to dust you shall return: turn away from sin and be faithful to Christ.' There is a sense in which the church needs to be always in Lent. That sense is that the church must always maintain a spirit of humility based on full, heartfelt and comprehensive repentance, not just for individual sins but for participation on corporate wrongdoing and societal injustice. The six traditional habits of Lent shape a congregation for the regular acts of humility that prepare it for an attitude of repentance in the way it recognizes its sins of evasion, justification, complicity and perpetration.

The first habit is self-examination: finding inside ourselves things that shouldn't be there, asking help from a trusted friend or pastor in calling on God to take them away and striving for them to be replaced by things that are there but have been neglected. The second habit is prayer: sitting still and putting oneself in the presence of God. Perhaps the most countercultural thing one can do. The third habit is fasting. Fasting is about power – about learning when and how to resist temptation, seduction, greed, idleness, envy. It means making a pattern of life so the smartphone doesn't become a transitional object; getting senses and self-control in better balance. Fasting means standing in solidarity with those who don't get to choose. If you can't give up a single meal, do you really care about global hunger? But fasting also means learning how to be really hungry: hungry for righteousness, for justice and peace; hungry, fundamentally, for Easter – hungry for the resurrection only God can bring in Christ.

The fourth habit is giving money away. There is never a time in life when it seems a good time to give money away. So it's good to set a time of year, a day of the week, for doing so – since it will never feel like the right time. It's best to tie money to prayers – to give money to something one believes in, and pray for the organization to which one gives money. The fifth habit is to read the Bible. Christians who use the word 'inclusion' or who long for a wider sense of God's mercy often despair that the Bible is frequently said to have a narrow perspective on the issues of the day. But they're often in no position to contradict such a view, because they know the Bible so little. There's only one way to change that. The Bible belongs to those who read it. You can never claim to have the Bible on your side if you don't know what it says.

The final habit is repairing broken relationships. This may mean making a small step in a large breach – or making a large step in a small breach. It could be cultivating a friendship across a social barrier of class, race or religion, or making a connection among people whose names you don't currently know, people from whom you're estranged without ever having done the damage yourself.

Renewal in the church isn't the final conquest by one party of all the other groups whose faith is flawed and whose practice is deficient. It's the discovery that God has given us everything we need – a discovery that only happens when we change from being the one who says, 'I thank you that I am not like others', to the one who says, 'God, be merciful to me, a sinner.' Renewal doesn't happen when one congregation decides it's self-sufficient and has no need of other Christians or other neighbours. It happens when a congregation has the humility to open its heart and see those who are doing its own work better than it does itself, and to open its mind and see the gifts God is sending it in the face of the stranger.

Becoming a blessing

Becoming a blessing is an apt summary of the argument of this book. For, what I am advocating is not so much a series of activities, let alone techniques, but more a state of mind. One congregation set about making a forward plan that envisaged where it would like to be in a few years' time and what steps it needed to take to get there. Through inviting ideas from members of the congregation, the leadership group arrived at 72 bright schemes for improving or adding or changing or beginning. Over an evening, the leadership group selected around 20 schemes that looked like they had sufficient practicality to be implemented, imagination to reflect the kingdom, authenticity to be true to the congregation's commitments, support to form a project oversight committee, and economy to be affordable.

Considering these 20 projects, the leadership group perceived they fell into three broad groups. Some could be regarded as building on existing initiatives: these they called 'deepening and broadening our programmes'. Others were new ideas that were true to the spirit of the community but as yet had no institutional home, and might if successful be floated off into a separate organization in their own right: these they called 'incubating new projects'. The third group were more about internal practices and procedures, like the welfare of employees and the recognition of unconscious bias: these they called 'becoming an exemplary organization'. Initially the leadership group had imagined a fourth category, more oriented towards positively influencing other organizations, entitled 'being a blessing'. But as the plan took shape, it became clear that all of the projects that might have sat in this fourth category better belonged under one of the other three headings. And gradually it dawned on the leadership group that simply by fulfilling their aspirations in the three agreed categories, their congregation would become a blessing. Because being a blessing meant no more than growing more faithful in more ways, and helping others do so; seeing green shoots of creativity and possibility, here and elsewhere, and fostering their development into maturity; and getting right the ways of living and working together, which brought out the best in everyone and made the community more than a sum of its parts, and walking with other communities as they sought to do the same.

And that was the moment that a new movement was born, whose ambition was no more and no less than to be a blessing to others and to help others bless others, and so imitate the action of God in Christ and anticipate the kingdom.

Notes

1 I'm grateful to Stanley Hauerwas for the idea of reading *Watership Down* as a political novel. See his 'A Story Formed Community: Reflections on *Watership Down*' in Stanley Hauerwas, *A Community of Character: Toward a Constructive Social Ethic* (Indiana: University of Notre Dame Press, 1986), pp. 9–35.

2 L. Gregory Jones, *Christian Social Innovation: Renewing Wesleyan Witness* (Nashville: Abingdon, 2016), p. 95.

3 Jones, p. 96.

4 Rob Goffee and Gareth Jones, *Why Should Anyone Work Here? What it Takes to Create and Authentic Organization* (Boston: Harvard Business Review Press, 2015), p. 14.

5 Goffee and Jones, p. 30.

6 Goffee and Jones, pp. 39–40.

Appendix:

Measuring the Kingdom

Existing models

The Bible is ambivalent about measurement. On the one hand, Ephesians expresses aspiration 'I pray that you may have the power to comprehend, with all the saints, what is the breadth and length and height and depth, and to know the love of Christ that surpasses knowledge, so that you may be filled with all the fullness of God' (Eph. 3.18). On the other hand, the census called by Emperor Augustus is clearly a sign of malign forces at work, and 1 Chronicles 21.1–8 records David's sin in seeking to number his people.

One widely acknowledged problem with counting is that what can't be counted doesn't count: such evaluation is reductionist, turning glory into commodity. But not all evaluation has to be simply a matter of counting what can be counted. And an individual or organization that regards itself as above or beyond evaluation is in constant danger of complacency and is missing out on opportunities to grow. It is also without evidence to convince members or funders that it is achieving what it is setting out to achieve. Resistance to measurement may be humility and attention to transcendent goods; but it may be laziness or reluctance to be held to account. Christ's ascension to the right hand of the Father affirms that God does not judge as the world judges; but Christ's incarnation suggests that the kingdom takes material form, and thus that some form of evaluation, even of the most devotional endeavours, is inevitable.

There are broadly two kinds of evaluation – quantitative and qualitative – the hard data of figures, and the soft information of surveys. Both depend almost entirely on what questions you ask. The hard data for a congregation might include average attendance at the main act of worship, across services throughout an average week or at Christmas and Easter; but it may also include baptism candidates, confirmation candidates, ordination candidates, participants in small groups, offering size and so on. Soft data may explore the quality of congregation members' engagement with the church, the depth of their experience, and change in their own lives perceived by themselves or others; but it may also investigate attitudes to the church from seekers, the lapsed, those of other faiths, of no professed faith, and tangible or intangible blessings experienced in the wider community whether as a result of or independent of church involvement.

Among evaluation tools widely used, the following may be relevant:

1 The Balanced Scorecard is a corporate model designed to recognize that financial performance is not the only significant measure of a company's success or well-being. In addition to financial outputs it adds three further metrics of organizational health: the customer perspective – whether customers are satisfied and retained; the internal process dimension of maximizing efficiency and quality; and the knowledge and innovation capacity, incorporating the need for learning and growth, adoption of technology and the culture of the organization. Each of the four criteria is measured by ultimate goals and key performance indicators that clock intermediate objectives.[1] This model is so widely used in commercial and charitable contexts that the question inevitably arises as to how it could be adapted for congregational performance.[2]

2 A Theory of Change is a causal model used by charities and funders to demonstrate the links between a proposed need,

activities, outcomes and impact. This will involve a process of simplifying the organization's work to as few steps as possible, producing a diagram linking their activities to their goals. The organization first states their goal, and works back from this to their outcomes, how they link to each other, and how their activities lead to said outcomes. Considering what else is needed externally reveals enabling factors. This complete framework assists in evaluating impact, by knowing which outcomes have to be measured and understanding how they are linked, and revealing what effect the initial activities and outcomes have.[3] New Philanthropy Capital, a charity think tank and consultancy, has free resources[4] on the theory of change and offers training and direct support for implementing one. This mechanism could be very useful for churches to map and evaluate projects and goals.

3   The case study of The Nature Conservancy highlights the need to crystallize your measurements to a minimum: after trialling a model with 98 measures, they settled on a simpler 'family of measures.' This measures success in mobilizing your resources, staff effectiveness on the job, and progress in fulfilling your mission – known as capacity measures, activity measures and impact measures. The impact is usually the most difficult, but usually the most crucial. The options for measuring a mission are by defining the mission to make it quantifiable, by investing in research to show that specific methods work, or by developing concrete microlevel goals that imply success on a larger scale.[5]

4   The LIGHT wheel (Learning and Impact Guide to Holistic Transformation) was produced by the charity Tearfund, influenced by work at the University of Bath. It has nine domains to measure well-being: personal relationships, emotional and mental health, physical health, participation and influence, environmental stewardship, material assets and resources, capabilities, living faith and social connections. The ground

it encounters constitutes the context: institutions, law, society, environment, technology, politics, services, security and economy.[6] It can be used throughout the project: as self-assessment for communities and churches, a reference framework and strategy development, a baseline assessment of a community or region, for monitoring a project, evaluating it and assessing impact. For impact assessment, it was embedded in another methodology – the Qualitative Impact Assessment Protocol (QuIP),[7] developed by the University of Bath Centre for Development Studies, and now curated by Bath Social and Development Research Ltd. The wheel has several strengths: its holistic nature, which includes faith; its ease of use; and adaptability throughout a project cycle. Just as Tearfund did, for a thorough impact assessment, it would have to be used with another assessment tool.

5   The Qualitative Impact Assessment Protocol, as introduced above and the name implies, uses qualitative data. It addresses some of the concerns and the tension between the two kinds of data: quantitative data often doesn't show the full social impact, yet good qualitative data can be expensive to produce and may not seem reliable. The intended beneficiaries are at the centre of this impact assessment, through individual interviews and group discussion. Their narrative is the raw qualitative data, which is analysed through a coding programme. This produces an awareness of the significant drivers of change, both positive and negative, and the complex relationships between these drivers and the outcomes.[8] This approach has been particularly used by larger-scale NGOs,[9] and the costs associated with commissioning the Bath Social and Developmental Research Ltd to produce a more rigorous and robust impact assessment would be more suited to a diocesan or national level.

6   The Transformational Index (TI) was established by Matryoshka Haus, a company working with social innovation and impact.[10] TI provides tools, products and services

to enable frontline social and supportive organizations to identify the key indicators of transformation, narrate their story of change and make a system of measurement.

a   Their workshop is a customizable tool, led by an experienced facilitator, guiding organizations through the process above. At the end, the organization receives a report with measurement framework. The Diocese of Leicester commissioned TI to assist them in evaluating the impact of projects receiving grants from their Growth Fund.[11]

b   TI also produces a self-facilitated project, Impact on Track, more suitable for smaller organizations beginning to consider impact, and those with discrete projects to evaluate. It is a guide for producing a method to gather appropriate data, to be used to assess and increase impact.[12]

7   Announcing 'A New Ministry Scorecard', Cameron Trimble notes that what matters is not a culture of evaluation but ensuring you measure the right things. Statistics about the millions of hits on your website or thousands of tweets per day are 'vanity metrics' that make you feel successful without gauging overall impact or longer-term success. Trimble is preoccupied with hard data. Among the appropriate subjects of measurement are: what proportion of people can articulate a clear sense of vision and purpose for the church; active participation in all areas of the life of the church, not just the principal act of worship; the number who are first-time guests, and the proportion of those who return a second time; the proportion of active participants below the age of 40; the proportion of externally focused ministry opportunities vis-à-vis internally focused management opportunities; the number of entry points into the faith community (e.g. website, small groups); the number of new ministries/churches started as church plants or satellite ministries; the number of community ministry partners; the proportion of the budget dedicated to ministry compared to building maintenance and mortgage; and the race, class and gender diversity of the worshipping community.[13]

8 Mission Action Plans, recommended by many dioceses in the Church of England, are an attempt to introduce strategic thinking into church life and have been adopted in a number of settings. They emphasize so-called SMART objectives – Specific (and Stretching), Measurable, Achievable, Relevant (and Realistic) as well as Time-bound (and Timely).[14] MAPs offer an introduction to strategic thinking about objectives and goals, but don't offer support in how a church might start to measure their objectives or know if their goals have been reached: they lack the key performance indicators of the Balanced Scorecard, or the clear causal links of a Theory of Change, so aren't as useful in establishing how a church is doing.

9 St Peter's Saltley Trust designed a survey to address the significant question, 'What helps disciples grow?'[15] Over a thousand churchgoers completed it, which identified two indicators to growth – depth of discipleship and strength of vocation – and four distinctive pathways to growth – group activity, Christian experience, church worship and public engagement.[16] The most important factor for growth was Christian experience, while public engagement increased depth of discipleship, and group activities increased strength of vocation, although these four pathways are not independent from each other.[17] The survey is not a method of evaluation of a church or project, like others listed here, yet its findings provide an important example of using indicators to assess a larger concept, and a guide to pathways and activities in developing faith.

10 Complementing Christian Schwarz's *Natural Church Development*, Robert Warren takes an entirely qualitative approach that encompasses seven marks of a healthy church, as follows: energized by faith, outward-looking focus, seeks to find out what God wants, faces the cost of change and growth, operates as a community, makes room for all, and does a few things and does them well.[18] Warren

defines healthy as wholeness, balance and harmony with God and all creation. Thus a healthy church is one that has been touched and energized by the presence of God so that it reflects something of the good news of the wholeness made possible through the knowledge of God as revealed in Christ by the Holy Spirit.[19]

There are important things to learn from each approach. Most obviously, the Balanced Scorecard insists that there cannot be just one metric for evaluation. Churches cannot use congregation size any more than companies can use end-of-year profits. A lot of the fears congregations have about evaluation stem from the concern that the criteria used will not do justice to the breadth and dimensions of what the church itself believes it is called to do, to be and to represent. A theory of change model would encourage a church to clarify its goal and to consider the causal links between activities, outcomes and impact. The family of measures approach recognizes that the more profound purposes are beyond measurement, but offers a way to address that problem by suggesting intermediate criteria ('concrete microlevel goals', rather like key performance indicators) by which one can establish if the initiative is along the right lines. The LIGHT wheel offers a framework for holistic evaluation, yet is accessible on a small scale. The Qualitative Impact Assessment Protocol shows that qualitative research can be robust and systematic, using the resources that technology offers. The Transformational Index offers support to those exploring impact measurement, and its providers also offer a service to assist in this process and have worked with faith organizations. Trimble's model of 'A New Ministry Scorecard' demonstrates how imaginative quantitative examination can be, but at the same time it shows the poverty of such analysis when used without accompanying qualitative research. Mission Action Plans are an important start for churches to think and plan for the long term, but a guide to measurement would be a vital addition. The example of the Saltley Trust shows that it is possible to answer significant spiritual questions, through creating indicators. Warren makes a huge step by substituting health for success. Since in the New Testament health and salvation are the same thing, this move is creative and welcome. His seven criteria are a manageable number and encouragingly broad. Moving entirely away from hard data is challenging and bold; it does however make it difficult to compare across contexts and to demonstrate progress.

A proposal for measuring a church

My proposal is for a model that distinguishes between grand-scale intangible goals ('see the kingdom come') and more immediate, recognizable indicators congruent with those goals ('establish one new ministry based on an incarnational vision'); to offer a balance of hard and soft forms of evaluation; and to do so across a spread of six contexts of healthy life and relationships: with God, with oneself, with God together (congregational life), with near neighbours (local mission), with unseen neighbours (national and global mission), and with the creation (actively engaging with non-human creation and passively reducing carbon footprint). An evaluation process such as this could be run on alternate years, with a core team unearthing the hard data and a wider consultation process exploring the soft data. The results should soon surface the areas that need attention in a strategic planning process.

A proposal for measuring a church

With God

Aim	Proximate Goals	Hard Metrics (e.g.)	Soft Impressions
Universal wholehearted discipleship	Those beginning in discipleship	# new to church # children # youth # enquirers' group # baptized/confirmed	Are you growing in faith? Are you seeing changes in your life? Are you telling your story differently?
	Those deepening discipleship	# in home groups # in intentional communities # in ministry training and # of whom are women, BAME, those with a disability, and other underrepresented groups # in service roles	Can you see the hand of God in adversity? Are you seeing the gifts God is bringing you? Are the Spirit's fruits growing in you?

Those regularly attending worship	# Sunday attendees # weekday attendees Level of voluntary giving	Is your faith central to your life? Is it shaping all your relationships and decisions? Is it expressed in prayer, study, giving, service, reflection, sacrifice and repentance? Have you taken a step of faith into a new challenge?
Those engaging the church's wider ministry	# attending lunch club # attending youth club	Do you have an awareness of God in your life? Does the church play any role in that?

Learnings

Starting with God affirms that Christianity is fundamentally about relationship. External measures are inadequate for measuring, but this is the territory where external metrics are most frequently applied – congregation size, growth, level of giving, number of youth, etc. It's important to distinguish between those new to faith, those going deeper, and those in between. But those in relationship with God and in whose life God is at work are by no means restricted to churchgoers.

With oneself

Aim	Proximate Goals	Hard Metrics (e.g.)	Soft Impressions
Universal embodiment of the fruits of the Spirit	Maintaining healthy bodies and lifestyles	# engaged in active self-care (e.g. nutrition/diet, exercise, counselling) # prepared for adversity (e.g. made a will, have life insurance, pension arrangements, savings)	How do you feel about your health and your body? Do you feel empowered to make changes that lead to greater health? How is your mental health? How is your self-esteem?
	Growing healthy relationships	# have good relationships with colleagues, neighbours and extended family # have made new friends in the last year # hopeful and pursuing reconciliation in fractured relationships	Do you trust the people with whom you spend most of your time, and could you turn to them in a crisis? Who have you learned most from in the last year?

Regular outlets for creativity	# engage in fine or performance arts, writing or sport # pursuing a course of study	What in life do you most enjoy? What have you learned in the last year?
Moments of wonder and joy	# experienced amazement in last month # can name recent achievement or fulfilment of long-held plans	What has moved you to profound emotion recently? Have you experienced 'heaven in ordinary'?

Learnings

This is a neglected area. Being in right relationship with oneself is surely a vital dimension of kingdom living. It is particularly challenging for hard metrics. But there are plenty of areas for softer ones. The questions might seem intrusive, but they illustrate how little most leaders know about the true well-being of their congregation members. Pastoral care is often more about this area than the other five.

With God together

Aim	Proximate Goals	Hard Metrics (e.g.)	Soft Impressions
A congregation that is one, holy, catholic and apostolic	Energized, diverse and dynamic	# programmes running besides worship Proportion of those with disability, BAME, LGBT+, no recourse to public funds, and other minorities in leadership and membership # leaders trained in Unconscious Bias # adjustments made to include all (e.g. wheelchair ramps, loop system, language of hymns revisited to recognize contemporary theological perspectives, BSL interpreting) # times services are in a different language # times senior lay leadership has changed hands and new leadership emerged	Do you feel God is 'moving in this place'? Is there a good balance of the old and the new, tradition and innovation? Is this a learning community? Is this a community of hope? Is this a community welcoming to all? Are times of conflict addressed through processes of reconciliation? A mystery worshipper can attend services one or more times as a critical friend to offer observations on whether the congregation is living up to its ideals, particularly concerning welcome and access.

Gathered in trust under God's guidance	Amount of time set aside for corporate prayer and discernment # times church took a corporate step of faith in God and one another in last 5 years Process of goal-setting and forward planning # people who can articulate goals and plans in general terms # trained in good safeguarding practice	Is the decision-making and governance theologically shaped and informed? Is there a good balance of risk and prudence?
Able to fund its ministry and mission	Healthy financial balance sheet Appropriate level of reserves Emerging areas of new income Healthy level of congregational giving Good stewardship of assets Staff paid the living wage Voluntarily producing a gender pay gap report Pension fund invested in an ethical scheme	Are you proud of the way your church raises and spends money? Does it feel like it's God's money? Is this expressed well in worship? Is money invested in line with the church's values?
Recognizable to the early church	Doing the things listed in Acts 2.42–7	Have there been moments when you've said of something that happened in your church, 'That can only have been the Holy Spirit'?

Learnings

This is where a huge amount of energy goes, and the temptation is always to concentrate on the hard metrics rather than the soft ones. There are some serious and valuable hard metrics and they are not to be neglected. Nonetheless, only the soft evaluation is likely to reach members' true sense of pride in and flourishing within a congregation. The most difficult things to assess are where the congregation is being faithful but doesn't feel good about it – for example, facing conflict and engaging in demanding processes of reconciliation with many setbacks and resentments, or making changes in leadership when leaders would prefer to stay in role indefinitely.

With near neighbours

Aim	Proximate Goals	Hard Metrics (e.g.)	Soft Impressions
That all should experience the presence and witness of the church as a blessing and through it glimpse the grace of God	Each congregation member pursuing vocation in mission in the world	# members who see their work/ life in the world as a calling # of different walks of life pursued by members Mapping of congregation members' work sectors and voluntary involvements	Do you see the work of your church as much in members' weekday lives as in Sunday activity? Do most of your members see their weekday lives as imitating or announcing the kingdom?
	In healthy relation to other churches of the denomination	At least one genuine partnership with another congregation Regular attendance at denominational gatherings	Does your church actively participate with a willing spirit in meetings and relationships with local churches of your denomination? Is your church working with local churches for the good of your denomination?
	Known, respected and cherished by the whole neighbourhood and seen as a sign of God's presence	# visits to website and social media responses # people who attend church vigils at times of national or local tragedy or anxiety	Would a survey of local residents, associations, charities and statutory agencies disclose such positive impressions? Would such a survey place a higher value on other local institutions or organizations?

| In constructive partnership with ecumenical, interfaith and secular neighbours to deepen relationships across divides and advance local projects | # of constructive local partnerships
# of members engaged in projects
combined hours of service
Concrete outputs of projects
places these projects have been replicated elsewhere | Is the whole neighbourhood coming together to address its challenges?
Is the church engaging in such a process in a humble spirit of partnership?
Is there a momentum and fellow feeling of organizing and seeing change for good? |

Learnings

It's important that at least three of the headings are concerned with the kingdom beyond the church. If a congregation surveyed a neighbourhood it might discover that fewer people were aware of the church's presence than they had imagined. Here the principle, 'You don't need to know everyone, but everyone needs to know you', applies. The key is for the church to be experienced as a blessing and not as self-absorbed, narrow-minded, arrogant or irrelevant. One way to show that is to partner with other agencies on projects rather than always to insist on facing every problem alone. Meanwhile, many churches will have incubated activities that have been spun off so that they are no longer run by the church but are a continuing legacy of the church in their community, often with continuing involvement and support of church members. These aspects of the long-term social and community impact of churches are often overlooked when not formally a part of a church's legal structure.

With distant neighbours

Aim	Proximate Goals	Hard Metrics (e.g.)	Soft Impressions
That the church should be part of networks seeking and seeing the coming of God's kingdom	Intentional prayer and engagement across culture, class, race and other divides	# of programmes # members involved Diversity of participants as a whole	Is the quality of engagement in keeping with the ethos of the church? Is this wholly or largely about advancing outcomes rather than the feel-good needs of participants? Is the congregation genuinely learning and refining its prayer and practice accordingly?
	Congregation exercising its collective strength to influence particular public issues for good	# members engaged in reflection and collective action # times positive outcomes achieved or effect tangible in shaping public	Are the issues genuinely about the common good, or self-serving? Has this involvement galvanized the congregation or individual members? Has reflection
		debate or consciousness # times Fairtrade products bought when possible	led to wiser engagement in the future?

	Support of organizations advancing kingdom causes overseas	# organizations supported Amount of money spent # hours of prayer and consciousness-raising	Has this been primarily about relationship and only secondarily about money? Has it reinforced stereotypes and power dynamics, or challenged them?
	Healthy relationship with the global denomination	# visits to global partners # references to global partners in worship or meetings	Are relationships based on genuine understanding or knee-jerk judgement? Has a way been found to enhance partnership even when there are ideological or cultural differences?

Learnings

This area is a test of the maturity of a congregation – whether it can believe in the presence and power of God in places where it can't itself see the difference its actions are making. It's also a test of whether it can stay with the complexity of problems and respect the wisdom and perspective of those who have been undergoing and working with these problems for a long time. A great many congregations have international programmes that are mainly for the benefit and satisfaction of congregation members themselves, or members have little or no regard for any impact, positive or negative, their engagement is having. This is an area for patience and humility.

With creation

Aim	Proximate Goals	Hard Metrics (e.g.)	Soft Impressions
All creation singing God's praise	Minimum ecological footprint	Kind and amount of energy used # changes introduced to reduce emissions (e.g. lightbulbs) # members who use renewable energy or public transport to get to church # bike racks available, % of waste recycled or composted	Does the congregation see this issue as integral to its discipleship? Does it make adjustments gladly or reluctantly?
	Appreciation for, awe towards and joy in creation	# church services relating to caring for creation # initiatives to increase biodiversity of church's green space	Are people experiencing joy at being a child of God? Are they at home in creation? Are they engaging directly with the non-human created world of animals, vegetables and minerals,

			and able to live without technological communication for significant periods?
	Adoption of sustainable lifestyles	# members who use renewable energy in home and on journeys # members who have adapted their diet and habits in line with green agenda	Are people finding they are becoming healthier, more grateful, more alive, more aware of the interdependence of creation?
	Partnering to advocate for sustainable economy	# members engaged in activism # times effects shown in policies or legislation or pronouncements	Does the congregation feel more aware of the gift of creation? Is there a momentum around making partnerships for change?

Learnings

It is important to emphasize that this area, best seen as part of discipleship rather than mission, is about experiencing God through the sacrament of creation, and only secondarily about the ecological crisis, pressing as that undoubtedly is. Neglect of creation deprives disciples of many avenues into the joy of God. An over-earnest insistence on lifestyle changes is unlikely to be relished unless it derives from prior gratitude for and enjoyment of creation.

Notes

1 www.balancedscorecard.org/BSC-Basics/About-the-Balanced-Scorecard.

2 Among those who have sought to do exactly this are J. C. Keyt, 'Beyond Strategic Control: Applying the Balanced Scorecard to a Religious Organization,' *Journal of Nonprofit and Public Sector Marketing* 8 (4) (2001): 91–102; L. Fry, L. Matherly and J.-R. Ouimet, 'The Spiritual Leadership Balanced Scorecard Business Model: vThe Case of the Cordon Bleu-Tomasso Corporation', *Journal of Management, Spirituality and Religion* 7 (4) (2010): 283–314; Noel Yahanpath, Philip Pacheco and Edgar A. Burns: 'Discussing a Balanced Scorecard for One Local Independent New Zealand Church', *Journal of Management, Spirituality & Religion* (2017); and S. Payer-Langthaler and M. Hiebl, 'Towards a Definition of Performance for Religious Organizations and Beyond', *Qualitative Research in Accounting and Management* 10 (3/4) (2013): 213–33.

3 Angela Kail and Tris Lumley, *Theory of Change: The Beginning of Making a Difference* (London: NPC, 2012), pp. 3, 5, 7–8.

4 www.thinknpc.org/themes/build-effective-charitable-organisations/theory-of-change/.

5 J. Sawhill and D. Williamson, 'Measuring what Matters in Nonprofits', *The McKinsey Quarterly* 2:2 (2001): 98–107; www.mckinsey.com/industries/social-sector/our-insights/measuring-what-matters-in-nonprofits.

6 Tearfund, *An Introductory Guide to the LIGHT Wheel Toolkit: A Tool for Measuring Holistic Change* (Teddington: Tearfund, 2016); Lydia Powell and Seren Boyd, *Fifty Years of Faith in Action: Learning and Insights* (Teddington: Tearfund, 2019), pp. 22–4.

7 *An Introductory Guide to the LIGHT Wheel Toolkit*, p. 14. Charlotte Flowers, *Flourishing Churches, Flourishing Communities: Church and Community Mobilisation in Uganda* (Teddington: Tearfund, 2018), frontmatter, pp. 14, 20.

8 http://bathsdr.org/.

9 http://bathsdr.org/about-bsdr/who-we-work-with/.

10 www.thetransformationalindex.org/.

11 www.thetransformationalindex.org/diocese-of-leicester-fund/.

12 www.thetransformationalindex.org/products/.

13 www.patheos.com/blogs/progressiverenewal/2012/05/a-new-ministry-scorecard.

14 For instance, on the Diocese of London page on MAPs: www.london.anglican.org/kb/mission-action-planning/.

15 www.saltleytrust.org.uk/whdg/.

16 Simon Foster, *What Helps Disciples Grow?* (Birmingham; Saltley Faith & Learning Series: 2 (Birmingham: Saltley, 2016). Leslie H Francis, Simon Foster, David W. Lankshear and Ian Jones, 'What Helps Christians Grow? An Exploratory Study Distinguishing among Four Distinctive Pathways', *Pastoral Psychology* (2019), https://doi.org/10.1007/s11089-019-00866-5.

17 Francis, Foster, Lankshear and Jones, 'What Helps Christians Grow?', p. 13.

18 See www.ncd-international.org/public/;jsessionid=C1FFA97C7DD 4262543ED3A9E43C9FA27, and Robert Warren, *The Healthy Churches' Handbook: A Process for Revitalising Your Church* (London: Church House Publishing, 2004).

19 Warren, *The Healthy Churches Handbook*, p. 15.

Bibliography

Balanced Scorecard Institute, www.balancedscorecard.org/BSC-Basics/ About-the-Balanced-Scorecard.

Bath Social and Development Research, bathsdr.org/.

Berry, Wendell, 'Two Economies', *Review and Expositor* 81 (2) (1984): 209–23.

Brueggemann, Walter, *Money and Possessions* (Louisville: Westminster John Knox Press, 2016).

Chesterton, G. K., *What's Wrong with the World*, first published in 1910.

Dichter, Thomas, *Despite Good Intentions: Why Development Assistance to the Third World Has Failed* (Boston: University of Massachusetts Press, 2003).

Eagleton, Terry, *Culture and the Death of God* (New Haven and London: Yale University Press, 2014).

Eliot, T. S. *Notes towards the Definition of Culture* (New York: Harcourt, Brace and Company, 1949).

Flowers, C., *Flourishing Churches, Flourishing Communities: Church and Community Mobilisation in Uganda* (Teddington: Tearfund, 2018).

Foster, Simon, *What Helps Disciples Grow?* Saltley Faith & Learning Series: 2 (Birmingham: Saltley, 2016).

Francis, Leslie H., Simon Foster, David W. Lankshear and Ian Jones, 'What Helps Christians Grow? An Exploratory Study Distinguishing among Four Distinctive Pathways', *Pastoral Psychology* (April 2019), https://doi.org/10.1007/s11089-019-00866-5.

Fry, L., L. Matherly and J.-R. Ouimet, 'The Spiritual Leadership Balanced Scorecard Business Model: The Case of the Cordon Bleu-Tomasso Corporation', *Journal of Management, Spirituality and Religion* 7 (4) (2010): 283–314.

Fujimura, Makoto, *Culture Care: Reconnecting with Beauty for our Common Life* (Downers Grove: IVP, 2017).

Giridharadas, Anand, *Winners Take All: The Elite Charade of Changing the World* (New York: Knopf, 2018).

Goffee, Rob and Gareth Jones, *Why Should Anyone Work Here? What it Takes to Create an Authentic Organization* (Boston: Harvard Business Review Press, 2015).

Goodchild, Philip, *Theology of Money* (London: SCM Press, 2007).

Hargaden, Kevin, *Theological Ethics in a Neoliberal Age: Confronting the Christian Problem with Wealth* (Eugene, OR: Cascade, 2018).

Hauerwas, Stanley, *A Community of Character* (Indiana: University of Notre Dame Press, 1986).

Hauerwas, Stanley, *Matthew* (Grand Rapids: Brazos Press, 2006).

Hauerwas, Stanley, 'How to "Remember the Poor"', in Stanley Hauerwas, *The Work of Theology* (Grand Rapids: Eerdmans, 2015), pp. 208–28.

Hirshfield, Jane, ed., *Women in Praise of the Sacred: 43 Centuries of Spiritual Poetry by Women* (New York: HarperCollins, 1994).

Ignatieff, Michael, *The Ordinary Virtues: Moral Order in a Divided World* (Cambridge, MA: Harvard University Press, 2017).

Johnson, Kelly, *The Fear of Beggars: Stewardship and Poverty in Christian Ethics* (Grand Rapids: Eerdmans, 2007).

Jones, L. Gregory, *Christian Social Innovation: Renewing Wesleyan Witness* (Nashville: Abingdon, 2016).

Kail, Angela and Tris Lumley, *Theory of Change; The Beginning of Making a Difference* (London: NPC, 2012).

Kelly, Colm and Blair Sheppard, 'Creating Common Purpose', *Global Solutions Journal* 1 (1) (2018): 80–7.

Kelly, Colm and Blair Sheppard, 'Common Purpose: Realigning Business, Economies and Society' (2017), retrieved from www.strategy-business.com/feature/Common-Purpose-Realigning-Business-Economies-and-Society?gko=e57f6.

Keyt, J. C., 'Beyond Strategic Control: Applying the Balanced Scorecard to a Religious Organization', *Journal of Nonprofit and Public Sector Marketing* 8 (4) (2001): 91–102.

London Diocese, Mission Action Planning, www.london.anglican.org/kb/mission-action-planning/.

Lupton, Robert D., *Toxic Charity: How Churches and Charities Hurt Those They Help, and How to Reverse It* (San Francisco: HarperOne, 2012).

Luther, Martin, 'The Large Catechism', in *Triglot Concordia: The Symbolical Books of the Evangelical Lutheran Church* (St Louis: Concordia, 1921).

Martin, Roger L. and Sally R. Osberg, *Getting Beyond Better: How Social Entrepreneurship Works* (Boston, MA: Harvard Business Review Press, 2015).

Milbank, John and Adrian Pabst, *The Politics of Virtue: Postliberalism and the Human Future* (London: Rowman & Littlefield, 2016).

Niebuhr, H. R., *Christ and Culture* (New York: Harper and Row, 1951).

NPC, www.thinknpc.org/themes/build-effective-charitable-organisations/theory-of-change/.

Payer-Langthaler, S. and M. Hiebl, 'Towards a Definition of Performance for Religious Organizations and Beyond', *Qualitative Research in Accounting and Management* 10 (3/4) (2013): 213–33.

Powell, Lydia and Seren Boyd, *Fifty Years of Faith in Action: Learning and Insights* (Teddington: Tearfund, 2019).

Reich, Rob, *Just Giving: How Philanthropy is Failing Democracy and How It Can Do Better* (Princeton: Princeton University Press, 2018).

Saltley Trust, www.saltleytrust.org.uk/whdg/.

Sawhill, J. and D. Williamson, 'Measuring What Matters in Nonprofits', *The McKinsey Quarterly* 2 (2) (2001): 98–107. www.mckinsey.com/industries/social-sector/our-insights/measuring-what-matters-in-nonprofits.

Snower, D., 'The Dangerous Decoupling' (2017), retrieved from www.g20-insights.org/wp-content/uploads/2017/05/The-Dangerous-Decoupling.pdf, p. 1.

Snower, D., 'Recoupling', *Global Solutions Journal*, 1 (1) (2018): 11–12.

Taylor, Charles, *A Secular Age* (Cambridge, MA: The Belknap Press of Harvard University Press, 2007).

Tearfund, *An Introductory Guide to the LIGHT Wheel Toolkit: A Tool for Measuring Holistic Change* (Teddington: Tearfund, 2016).

Transformational Index, www.thetransformationalindex.org/; www.thetransformationalindex.org/diocese-of-leicester-fund/; www.thetransformationalindex.org/products/.

Trimble, Cameron, 'A New Ministry Scorecard', www.patheos.com/blogs/progressiverenewal/2012/05/a-new-ministry-scorecard.

Tye, Joe, '12 Reasons Culture Eats Strategy for Lunch', www.slideshare.net/joetye/12-reasons-culture-eats-strategy-for-lunch-25988674/73-The_Cultural_Blueprinting_Toolkit_features.

Warren, Robert, *The Healthy Churches' Handbook: A Process for Revitalising your Church* (London: Church House Publishing, 2004).

Wells, Samuel, *Speaking the Truth: Preaching in a Pluralistic Culture* (Nashville: Abingdon, 2008).

Wells, Samuel, *Learning to Dream Again: Rediscovering the Heart of God* (Grand Rapids: Eerdmans, 2013), pp. 72–8. UK edition, with substantial alterations, Norwich: Canterbury Press, 2013, pp. 61–7.

Wells, Samuel, *A Nazareth Manifesto: Being with God* (Oxford: Wiley-Blackwell, 2015).

Wells, Samuel with David Barclay and Russell Rook, *For Good: The Church and the Future of Welfare* (Norwich: Canterbury Press, 2017).

Wells, Samuel, *Incarnational Ministry: Being with the Church* (Grand Rapids and Norwich: Eerdmans and Canterbury Press, 2017).

Wells, Samuel, *Incarnational Mission: Being with the World* (Grand Rapids and Norwich: Eerdmans and Canterbury Press, 2018).

Wilde, O., 'The Soul of Man Under Socialism' (1891), retrieved from www.marxists.org/reference/archive/wilde-oscar/soul-man/.

Williams, Raymond, *Keywords*, rev. edn (New York: Oxford University Press, 1983).

Williams, Rowan, *Grace and Necessity: Reflections on Art and Love* (London: Morehouse Publishing, 2005).

Yahanpath, Noel, Philip Pacheco and Edgar A. Burns, 'Discussing a Balanced Scorecard for One Local Independent New Zealand Church', *Journal of Management, Spirituality & Religion* (2017).

Index of Names and Subjects

CPSIA information can be obtained
at www.ICGtesting.com
Printed in the USA
LVHW090422261119
638554LV00001B/106/P